HOW TO WRITE
A NOVEL

An Anthology of 20 Craft Essays About Writing,
None of Which Ever Mention Writing

edited by
Aaron Burch

autofocus books
Orlando, Florida

Published by Autofocus Books
PO Box 560002
Orlando, Fl 32856
autofocuslit.com

Essay Anthology
ISBN: 978-1-957392-25-7

Cover Illustration ©Amy Wheaton
Library of Congress Control Number: 2023940704

HOW TO WRITE
A NOVEL

An Anthology of 20 Craft Essays About Writing,
None of Which Ever Mention Writing

Table of Contents

ON PERSEVERANCE

ON LIVING A WRITING LIFE

INTRODUCTION

Aaron Burch

Talking about writing—talking about any art, really—is tricky. To focus too much on craft can start to feel formulaic, can feel like it removes the art part of the equation. The best and most memorable stories break all kinds of rules and suggestions, of course. On the other hand, to not talk about the craft of it at all can start to sound too magical and woo-woo, ignoring the work that went in, the considerations, the decisions made along the way.

In between those two hands is that sneakily fine line where art resides. The result of studying and thinking about and considering everything a piece of writing can do all while leaving space for, and acknowledging, the magic can (and, most often, will) happen when the subconscious picks up where that studying and thinking and considering leaves off, or by accident, or when only trying to entertain yourself, or, maybe most common of all, *just because.*

*

This anthology—like a lot of my best ideas, many of which are dumb ideas and/or tossed off jokes turned into real things that, in retrospect, get reclassified as best ideas—started as a tweet:

I would like to edit a "how to write a novel" craft book anthology with essays about skateboarding & houseplants & making art & 70s paranoid thrillers & going to the driving range & petting zoos & road trips & naps & tattoos &..., and it never mentions writing.

Did I really want to do this? I don't know. It was somewhere between, and/or simultaneously both, sincere and snarky.

But then it turned into a real thing, this thing you're reading right now, and I gotta say, I think it turned into something kind of magical.

*

Speaking of tossed off tweets turned into real things, a year or two ago, I tweeted:

I can't remember the last time a journal solicited me for a story, it's maybe been years, but three journals have asked about skull paintings in the last month or so, which is kinda weird but rad but also weirdly dumb and funny but also also super fun and rad?

Was I fishing for a solicitation? Probably. Was I also just bragging about my art, which I'd only recently gotten into? Almost certainly.

And, an editor friend did in fact reach out and solicit a flash piece of cnf, which felt encouraging, but I didn't have anything. I love to be asked though, and sometimes a prompt can turn into something fun and great, so I went to work. With that tweet in mind, I started thinking about my paintings, and how in even only six months or so, I'd already gotten so much better. In general, but especially with what I drew most often: skulls. How, at first, I'd needed to look at a reference image with every little line I drew, but then, over time, with each new skull I drew, I needed to less and less often, until I didn't need to at all. That led to thinking about all kinds of other activities and skills and hobbies or whatever where some version of that basic principle had proved to be true—running, cooking, skateboarding.

When I finished and sent it to said soliciting editor friend, she replied that I had "somehow wrote a craft essay that isn't an awful craft essay, but is actually really beautiful and authentic." Am I quoting that here to egotistically brag? A little. But mostly to highlight how I had not only not intended it as a craft essay, but had never even thought of it as such. Maybe, probably that was why it could be said to be beautiful and authentic. It had happened by accident, because I was really only trying to entertain myself, *just because*.

*

Here's an anecdote I've told before: When I first started teaching, I asked a handful of friends who were teachers for suggestions, pep talks, reassurance, advice. Any and everything they could share. One told me she started every section of her comp class by reading a short poem. She said she didn't talk about it, didn't analyze it, it wasn't really in any way related to the day's lesson plan. It just acted as a kind of signal that class had started; that, among other things, they were there to think and talk about language and communication. I loved the idea, and loved her reasoning and thoughtfulness, and so borrowed it myself. And for the first few weeks of my first semester teaching, I started my comp classes by poem. Only, she was something of a poet, she loved poetry, she had arrived at this strategy through thinking about her own process, whereas I'm something of a moron when it comes to poetry, feel awkward reading it aloud, and had borrowed her strategy and thinking about my own. I liked the idea though, and I thought about this collection of quotes I'd collected from interviews that I called "on writing," and sometimes they were indeed writer quotes about writing, but even more often they were from baseball players or rappers, directors or standup comedians, chefs and magicians, all talking about their process. So I started reading one of those at the top of ever class. And it immediately felt more natural.

It turns out, maybe my favorite way of thinking and talking and listening to and reading about the process of writing is by people talking about their process regarding anything they care about that isn't writing. Here's a book of that.

On Finding Your Voice

TAKE IT STEEZY
Scott Mitchel May

I skate Mongo. Most skaters kick using their back foot so that their front foot is always in position to make minimal adjustments when doing a trick. Which is to say I use my front foot, the foot which is normally planted at the front of the deck and used primarily to ollie and do flip-tricks, to kick and propel myself, swinging it all the way back around and getting it back on the front of the deck before doing a trick. Hyper inefficient.

Mongo is short for mongoloid (skaters historically being not just insensitive in the terminology used when naming tricks and stances but purposefully so; see also the Ghetto Bird (a trick perfected by Kareem Cambell), the Sex Change, and The Mute Air (first done by deaf skater Chris Weddle who could, by all accounts, speak)) because you'd have to be fucking stupid to skate mongo.

I skate mongo because it feels right and it feels comfortable and it feels like I can generate a lot of speed in a really short amount of time. That and when you swing your front foot all the way around at full speed and have to set up as quickly as you can to ollie and clear the edge of the box, or get up on the ledge, or even just plant your foot to hit a bank, it feels more dangerous, and to me, that feels better. It hits the dopamine charge I am looking for. My skating style is sketch as fuck and that's where the fun is. That's my style.

That's my steeze. Steeze is style + ease because you need to have both to make what you do look effortless, to look cool, to look like you don't care when you care very much. My steeze is slightly out of control.

I can skate fast and sketch and sloppy and not fall a whole lot. I've found my lane and I am in it. I am too old to be getting up on handrails or going for big ledges or huge stair sets anyway. I am not turning pro at forty.

There is a certain peace and a certain calmness when you accept what you are capable of and what you are not. There is happiness in knowing that you have a style, that you can go hard, that you have some steeze. It can only be gained by doing the thing for years and years and years. You can drop it for over a decade and when you come back to it your steeze is still there. The legs remember. You can stand on your board and your whole body seems to just go right back to where it was then. You won't have your tricks, but those come back with time. You have the more important thing. You have your style. You can't teach it to a person. You can teach them to ollie, you can teach them to boardslide, you can show them how to drop in and then watch them bottom out on their first attempt and then laugh at them and hand them a beer, but you can't tell their legs how to be. You can't put comfort in their muscles.

Because I'm old I get up early and I go to the Goodman Skatepark on the east side of Madison, WI pretty much when it opens at 8 AM most weekdays, and I am usually the first one in. I really only started skating again after a long hiatus last summer. But I wasn't hardcore about it then. I am now. The other 30 - 40 somethings show up between 9 and 11. We are of varying skill levels.

Sunny shows up about an hour after I do. He is 40 and picked it back up five years ago and is by far the most technically sound of the old-heads. He's got that proficient style. That practiced and precise control. This makes sense for Sunny because he is a Professor in the School of Engineering at The University. He's got a dozen or so tricks that he can do all over the park and on obstacles of varying difficulty, on lock. It's impressive to watch Sunny skate because he's figured out how it all works and has made it his business to make it look easy. He falls as much as anyone doing the more technically difficult shit, but his makes are clean. His style is organized. He's got his thing. I like watching Sunny skate because his style is so opposite to my own, and I really like when Sunny almost falls because Sunny is always on the right side of out of control, but when he almost falls but pulls it out anyway, he's just on the wrong side of out of control, and that, to me, is where skating is. That's not where skating is for Sunny. And that's okay.

Sometimes Sunny will tell me when I am landing a trick but not doing it technically correct and proper and I tell him I didn't start skating because I was super good at doing things technically correct and proper. He understands but judges me a little, and that's okay too. People are going to do that when your style is that of an insane, adrenaline-punched, mongo-footed maniac.

I am relearning ledge 50-50s on the low box at the park. I haven't done one since 2006. My process for learning a trick is to try and do it slowly at first, rolling up and getting on, then not having the speed, and just sort of falling off. I get frustrated with this after about three attempts and then just start doing it at speed. I don't think about my feet or what they have to do. I just push hard and throw myself at the thing, and throw myself at the thing, and throw myself at the thing until I get one. Then I try to remember what that felt like — getting one. I try to remember what it felt like when my trucks hit the ledge, how they bit in and slowed at impact, how my body had to adjust, and how I came off. Did I roll off the end lifting the nose of my board, or did I pivot off in the middle? I try to remember how it felt to roll away, after. The relief. It's a feeling I try to hold onto, but I never can. The way I learn anything is I need to train my brain to crave the moment of reward and then accept the fact that the moment will leave and then I just have the rote thing I can now do, refining it until it fits my style.

I can't teach anyone how to do anything because my advice is always the same: you just set out to do it and then you do it. If you like it enough, if it is rewarding to you personally enough, you will keep throwing yourself at the ground in pursuit of that reward. It will feel too good not to keep going. It's the only explanation I have for why anyone does anything. And when it feels good enough to keep doing it enough to get even marginally good at it, then the rewards become better and faster and more immediate. Then style starts to take over. Then ease. Then you can put it down in 2006 after someone steals your board at a party and you can't afford another one and not pick it up again until 2021 and still be able to skate mongo as fast as you can at a bank and not look or feel stiff or be afraid because you know you can do it because you've always done it.

The point is, it all works if it works, and that's a beautiful thing. It's a thing you can't expect in many other pursuits.

Someone will tell you this is how it's done and you kinda have to listen because you care and you want to succeed. But there is freedom in skating when you are old because succeeding has no meaning. You won't get sponsored. You won't make money. So you say fuck it and you do it the way you want and it spikes that feeling that you can't replicate unless you are doing something you love exactly the way you want to do it. It's amazing. Your steeze becomes why you do it. Not impressing the others at the park. Not hitting that huge gap. Not landing that kickflip you've been working on. Those are all things that are temporary and fade and are gone the moment you touch them. The pursuit of steeze is evolving and eternal and can't be touched. Its rewards are evergreen.

Style, once earned, never fades.

RECIPE FOR AN AUTHENTIC, FROM SCRATCH SHEPHERD'S PIE (WHEN I DON'T HAVE LAMB IN THE FRIDGE)
Donald Ryan

But I do have ground turkey we got at a reduced price thawed from the freezer. And there's those last few potatoes I need to do something with. They're not growing eyes, not yet, but even if they were there'd still be a decent portion of salvageable potato. A frozen bag of mixed veggies is a golden ticket. Meaning I'm on my way to something. With timing and seasonings and a childlike joy of cooking this something could even become a damn fine dish. Doesn't have to be the greatest. As long as it's tasty. Tasty is edible. Tasty is a happy plate.

This is how I go into dinner every night. I survey what's already there, survey the fridge and pantry. Look for things that might be nearing the end of their shelf-life. Take stock and compose. I might pull a few items out and line the counters. Might preheat the oven. But I don't cook. Not yet. I concoct. There's a meal in this kitchen somewhere. I just have to find it.

My wife cannot work like this. The opposite, she prefers to bake. The preciseness of the recipes, outlined and set, when followed yielding an exact result. So, needless to say, when she plans to make dinner, it's been preplanned. We'll be in the store and she'll think it would be nice to have a specific meal soon, so we set out to gather those specific ingredients. Then within a week's time she'll make that meal as she set out to do, and it will taste great, exactly as intended. This works for her. For her, it's perfect.

I'm chaos. My mind is a Where's Waldo looking for the scroll and the glasses and Wizard Whitebeard if the scroll is creativity and the glasses are exploration and the wizard is experimentation making it so if I'm lucky on this journey I'll happen upon Waldo thus making Waldo a tasty treat worth sharing. Ok, convoluted metaphor. But the idea is there. Or will be. Just like the ingredients my wife didn't use all of in her dish which I've now pulled out and lined atop the counter in a semblance of order I'll eventually order along the way.

Which brings me to prep work. Prep work is underrated. With a destination in mind, people want to get there. I get it, me too; I want to eat. But you can't rush the process. It's science. No dish can be made without it. Take even a pre-fab frozen pizza. Bare minimum, still have to open the box.

I don't take the herbs and vegetables I chop and spices I plan to use and line them in tiny saucers I may or may not have taken from various restaurants over the years as if my making dinner is a cooking segment. That's a waste of time and effort. The more bowls used only means more bowls to clean. Why divvy out salt? Fuck all that. Should salt to taste, anyway. But! What there does need to be is some sort of method or flow. A leads to B. X leads to Y. 1 leads to 2. One thing, one tiny manageable thing, leads to the next. Otherwise, worrying about the 24 other letters, let alone $\infty - 2$, that's stress. But peeling potatoes leads to dicing potatoes. Diced potatoes leads to a pot of salted water. Boiling potatoes leads to browning the ground turkey. You're on your way to getting there.

So, the potatoes are boiled and strained. The ground turkey is browned and strained. Time it right, use the same strainer. Time it more right, use the same pot. I have one of those square, red copper ones because every job needs some tools. So after dumping the strained potatoes into a mixing bowl, I give that copper bad boy a wipe down and throw the turkey in because I really hate washing more dishes than I must. Dirtying dishes comes with the territory, but why make more work for myself? Already put in an eight hour shift. And even a simple meal is creating, and creating, in and of itself, is work. I get done what needs to be done without working myself into the ground. Try not to scorch, try not to burn, try not to burn out. That's not fun for anyone. Because at the end of the day, as is the timing for dinner, I'm setting the task therefore it's pivotal I set forth with some degree of love—otherwise, what's the point of doing? Take French techniques. That fancy shit thrives on effort. Not in the number of dishes that can be piled in the sink. (To reiterate, there's absolutely no reason in portioning salt into a tiny saucer.) However, the inverse of this is also true: use as many utensils, dishes, and *-er* ending appliances necessary to complete the task at hand.

Anyway, so the potatoes are boiled and strained. The ground turkey is browned and strained. The foundation, thus, is laid. The time to go through and build layers and complexities and ensure every component is equally as perfect as it can be made to be has arrived. My go to, at a barest of bare minimums, is the holy trinity of salt, pepper, and garlic. These three alone can balance almost any dish. My worst-case scenario is salt alone. But even then, with the right focus and play on natural flavors, palatable can be accomplished. All other herbs and spices then, even for the most serious of dishes, are experimentation, play, and fun. If you are what you eat then dinner inherently becomes an extension of you. Treat it as such.

The greatest cook I've ever worked with was a sous-chef who didn't realize he was the best cook I'll ever work with.

(Long story short:) Part of the menu involved a daily corn muffin. That's a different muffin every day. That's a whole shitload of corn muffins. One morning, we had some kiwis left over from a cheesecake, we had herbs like always, so I throw out, "what about basil-kiwi corn muffins," inflected with a question mark. His response was a phrase I guarantee he had no idea would stick with me in nearly every, and not just culinary, aspect of my life. "In the right proportions everything goes together." Well, shit. He's not wrong.

That said, ideally, for a mash, there should be a little milk or cream to help as a binder. Here, we don't have either. We have butter. And we have mayonnaise. Salt, pepper, garlic. We have ranch, doable, yes, but overkill—it's equally as important to know when to hold back. There's an onion. Dice it. Throw it in that square, copper pot to sweat in a little butter while blending and whipping and tasting the potatoes. When glistening towards translucent, the meat's going back in. Salt. Pepper. And the garlic? Generously splash in Worcestershire sauce (the garlic's in there). Find some sage in the cabinet. Sure. Rosemary, too. A pinch. Dump in that bag of veggies microwaved for six minutes as opposed to the recommended seven. Let that simmer to meld flavors. Taste. Add more salt. Taste. More Worcestershire because why not. Taste. Dollop a scoop of those now mashed potatoes to thicken without the use of flour. Tweak and fine tune, but don't overdo. Some steps cannot be retraced. So, tread till it can be eaten alone. That's when to stop.

This doesn't happen on the first go in a kitchen. Those green will go too far. Other than eating and loving to eat, I wasn't born with some innate culinary ability. And I'd never claim to be an expert. But I did spend well over a decade deep in the shit. Bars. Fast casuals. Fine dining. Tourist traps. No formal education, just experience and on the fly training. Even now, out of the game, these days as a small-town librarian of all the least likely things, I still push myself in the kitchen. Experiment. Make the best dishes I can although 99% of the time they're only for my wife and I. I do this for me. Even when flavors don't come out right or a sauce doesn't nappe, I push to see what I did right and to see what I could do better. There's no attempting success without the occasional fuck up. And more often than not, I'm surprised by how much I get right and how many things unintentionally come out better than my limited knowledge could fathom.

Back to the stovetop before it scorches: The pieces have been prepared, tinkered with, and tested. Time to polish. Me, I've got options. If it's a larger quantity of meat/potatoes, I'll use the same red, copper pot and layer the mash atop what's already in the pot. If the amount requires some height, I'll layer in a loaf pan. Use what works best for the ingredients. Form follows function. Determine the best option either way, stack it up, smooth it out, give it the look you want, and finish it off in the oven.

But wait, where's the cheese? Well, Gordon Ramsey never uses cheese on his shepherd's pie. This is my wife and I's justification. Really, we don't have any because we've cut most dairy from the house.

Anyway, with it in the oven, wash the potato bowl, the beaters, the copper pot if you went with the loaf pan. Leave out the rubber spat, used to stir the turkey and to smooth the potato layer, for serving. Take a moment, tidy up. Things are roasting. Can't rush an oven. This time is given, use it. That sous chef I admire was also in the habit of saying, "Keep it tight," as a key component to any task. The flavors or knife-work or technique can be complicated but there should be a flow and simplicity that makes it seem like it was done with ease. Cooking anything, by default, is systematic. Keep it tight. And since the dish is still finishing, another digression: Find people you admire, even if it's never face to face. Learn from them; have them teach you whether it's their intention or not. Pick up insight any place you can. Eat widely. Taste as much as you can, in as many combinations as you can. Pick out the most unusual items on a menu, pick an item you know you can't make at home, dissect it, but don't forget from time to time to return to favorites and comforts. There's a world to consume. It's sustenance. Mimic your discoveries. Then forge your own flavor profiles. And have fun for fuck's sake. You don't have to enjoy it every step of the process—cooking is tiring, the heat sucks, cleaning with a sliced finger is a tiny torture—but having created be proud you created, even if your timing was bit off and the bottom scorches. You'll know for next time. Make sure there is a next time. Eat every day.

Time's up.

Personally, after twenty minutes or so of setting in the oven, if the top of the potatoes aren't browned to my liking (more for a visual aesthetic than anything), I'll switch the oven to broil for a few. It's not necessary. I do it for me. I recommend doing your version for you. It's your dish.

A dish which is finally out of the oven. Ready to plate. Ready to serve.

Ready for the final step. At least for me. Through the years of many shared meals, I have a good sense of my wife's tastes. Know there's some things I'd chow contentedly which she couldn't palette. I trust her. So I might ask her opinion on a dish or a component. Especially if I try something new. It's valuable information. What works? What doesn't? What can I do better? And importantly, what was enjoyable which can be further improved upon? Now: I don't make this the focal point of dinner conversation. That's obnoxious. Sure, there are times, as a husband, I actively choose to be annoying; but obnoxious serves no benefit. So I'll ask a simple question. I'll listen to the answer. And I watch. What was finished, what wasn't, was something eaten with vigor or completed first? It's like telling a joke. Someone might say it's funny, but if they don't laugh, then is it? This is the necessity of trust. If it sucks, she'll tell me. It's crucial. However, the flip side to this coin is if the dish is served to others, friends or family, those outside of the hub that is my wife and I. Never ask them. Still watch. But never ask. Your job is done. They're served. It's on their plate and out of your hands. Allow them, without your inter-ference, to have their experience. If they compliment the food say thank you without listing the insecurities that went into the recipe. Simultaneously, take these compliments with a grain of salt. Salt makes everything better.

Enjoy.

FERMENTING HOT SAUCE
or, your life is love and that's worth sharing
e rathke

A layer of mold. The question rises: do I throw it out or scoop it off and let it keep fermenting.

Sandor Ellix Katz wrote the bible on fermentation and he never let a bit of mold ruin a good fermentation. And when someone writes a bible, you may as well pay attention. Not wanting to toss out all those peppers, the onions, garlic, and pineapple, or lose the few days of fermentation, I scooped it off and threw it out, let the hot sauce continue fermenting.

This was my first attempt at making hot sauce. I made the slightly unusual step of blending everything together first, and then letting the fully formed sauce ferment. Or, half of it. I left the other half fresh and refrigerated it right away. The flavor had a simplicity to it. It was juicy and yellow, with a real fruit forward punch followed by the heat, which rose from the back of my throat and up into my mouth, my nose. The pound of serrano peppers made my sinuses burn in a dry and unpleasant way. My eyes watered at that first taste and I coughed in a way that reminded me of my cat sneezing. Even so, it went well on tacos, in eggs, on pizza, hotdogs, burgers, chicken wings, and just about anything else.

Fermentation had a strange appeal to me. All the work was frontloaded. Toss it in a big jar, put a lid on it lightly, cover the jar with a towel to keep the light out, and forget about it for a week or two. With that first batch, I never was able to really forget it. Every time I walked through my kitchen—roughly 100 times a day—the hot sauce pulled at me. Its tiny hooks in my skin dragging me over to check on it, make sure it was still...what? Fermenting?

The first few days revealed nothing no matter how often I checked. As the days went on, I saw the bubbles forming until it became like a churning cauldron that, by the sixth day, had settled. Which was when the mold appeared.

Having tasted the unfermented version of the hot sauce, I was impatiently waiting for the fermented version to finish. Of course, finish, with regard to fermentation, has more to do with the fermenter than the food fermenting.

There's no indicator on your hot sauce or pickles or kimchi that lights up letting you know the food has reached appropriate levels of fermentation. There are no uniform looks for fermented food that you can compare what you have before you to some Platonic Ideal. Fermentation is a squishy, messy, imprecise process. You'll feel the need to tinker, to adjust, but what it really needs is time. How much time?

Well, that depends on you, buddy.

A week was about all I could handle, especially after the potentially disastrous mold growth. I brought out the fresh hot sauce to compare. Take a spoonful of one and then the other. To get a real sense of comparison, I wanted to try the fresh stuff again. But deeper inside me was this desire to taste the fermented hot sauce undiluted by other flavors.

And so I led with the untasted, untested, possibly poisonous fermented sauce.

Even before taking the spoonful in my mouth, I noticed the difference. The smell less sharp, more balanced with the citrus. I held it in my mouth for a moment like I was tasting wine rather than hot sauce. The flavor was still fruit forward, but with less of a punch. The pineapple had mellowed as it fermented, but also pulled closer to the bell peppers, the garlic. The flavors had more depth. Where the fresh sauce had had a shallowness to it that I didn't recognize at the time, the fermentation revealed complexity to flavors I believed singular and clear. Yes, there was a muddiness to where one flavor became another, how the flavors twisted and contorted one another against my tongue. But this was not really messiness. This was something new. A melding, pulling the many flavors into a single flavor rich with sound and shape. Even the texture of the sauce seemed bolder, more robust. Thicker rather than thin and watery. The heat, rather than trailing behind to knife at my sinuses, rose gently like the swell of a wave. Milder, certainly, but also more well-rounded.

I tasted the fresh sauce for the last time that day. It would go abandoned in my refrigerator until I eventually tossed it out.

It had gotten moldy.

From there, I fermented everything. Fermented with different flavors, with different goals. Some were horrible mistakes while others were glorious. Even made a batch of mead that went surprisingly well. So well that I made two more. But always I kept coming back to hot sauce. The serrano had been too mild once fermented and so I bought a pound of habanero peppers, used mango to cut through the spice, then bell peppers, onions, and garlic to add body. This time, I fermented the vegetables first, roughly chopping them and using baking weights to keep them submerged in the salinized water. I set them aside for two weeks and impatiently waited.

Again, I found myself obsessively checking on the sauce nearly every day. Found myself thinking of things I could have done differently. Different peppers, different vegetables.

Maybe carrots would have added some nice texture to the sauce. Maybe a pound of habanero was too much for me.

After two weeks, I blended the vegetables with mango and went straight to tasting.

The texture was just glorious. Something about the flesh of the fresh mango melding with the fermented vegetables created a thickness to the sauce. The habanero, rather than overwhelming me, made me appreciate its heat and subtlety for the first time. The sauce was neither heat nor fruit forward but a symphony of notes rising together to fill my mouth with exactly what I hoped to achieve. No, it was better than that.

My imagination had been too small, too timid.

The sauce itself grew beyond me, pulled me along to follow in its shade.

I put it on everything. Any kind of food you can eat got a dollop of my hot sauce. It was perfection.

And yet, the next time I went to make hot sauce, I iterated once more. The fun of food was its endless flexibility. Why keep making the same thing? If I could accidentally make sauce this good, imagine how much better it could be with some more deliberation and intention.

And so I tinkered. Changed ratios and even used different peppers and fruit. Tried scorching the peppers before fermenting them or even just roasting them. I tried dozens of techniques, adjusting this and that. And while the sauce was almost always good—excepting one or two batches—I never found the perfect melding of flavors, body, and spice that I had stumbled into so blindly.

I love to experiment with flavors and techniques, with ingredients. But I had a lifetime of eating food, of making food. Often, I've found, that I'm at my best when I think less and just let my tastebuds guide me. Yes, technique and experience had made me incomparably better, but it had, in some ways, polluted my instincts.

I knew what good food was. I knew what I liked. More than that, I knew what people liked. And, ultimately, we cook for others. Yes, there's a pure joy in cooking the perfect meal for yourself, but it will never rival the pleasure of a meal shared between friends, between lovers, between family.

Thus and so, I stopped being so clever about it all. I chopped my veggies, my peppers, and dropped them into a big jar to ferment in salinized water. Then, I waited.

I continue to wait, allowing all that I've learned, all that I've loved, to come bubbling together inside me, leading me towards a more perfect sauce.

ABOUT THAT TIME I SOLD MY COPIES OF THE FIRST THREE AMERICAN ANALOG SET RECORDS WHEN I REALLY, TRULY SHOULDN'T HAVE, AND HAVE REGRETTED IT EVER SINCE

James Brubaker

There's something like a joke in *High Fidelity*, Hornby's novel, I think, though maybe the film, too—I'm not sure, having neither read nor watched either in at least fifteen years—about Rob Gordon organizing his record collection "autobiographically." It's an absurd idea, enough to make a record collector feel a little queasy. How would one find anything, ever? How much more complicated would it be just to put a record back on the shelf after listening to it? I'm not even sure where half of my records would fit to begin with: when I first encountered an album or artist, or the point when an album had the greatest impact on my life? It's an interesting thought experiment—would I file Elvis Costello's *All This Useless Beauty* in the high school/1996 section, when I first purchased it on CD but rarely listened to it because it was too "soft," or in the contemporary section where it slots into regular rotation for late night listening sessions? What about Stereolab, whose discography through 1999 I listened to more than was probably healthy for about two years in college, but who I then put more-or-less aside for twenty years until rediscovering them during Covid lockdowns? Or what about Steely Dan?—I listened to *Aja* for about three months in 1992, having borrowed the CD from my local library a couple of times, only to then get into punk and decide I hated Steely Dan's professionalism and polish for thirty years before suddenly, inexplicably falling madly in love with them when I turned forty, as if some genetic switch for middle aged men were abruptly flipped. Undoubtedly, organizing a record collection autobiographically is a wildly impractical proposition. But it's fun to think about because there's an interesting idea threaded into the premise: A record collection can, and maybe should—though who am I to tell anyone what their record collection *should* do—tell a story about its owner, its curator.

Here's a story about mine, and to get there, let's return to the previous thought experiment—where would I file the first three American Analog Set records, *The Fun of Watching Fireworks, From Our Living Room to Yours,* and *The Golden Band,* issued by Emperor Jones in 1996, 1997, and 1999, respectively? I purchased the third one first, at Everybody's Records in Cincinnati, when it came out in July of 1999, within months of starting to collect records. When I was back in Bowling Green for school that fall, regularly making record shopping excursions into Michigan, I grabbed the other two at Wazoo Records in Ann Arbor. I played each album at least a hundred times, chain smoking cigarettes and reading, or playing video games, or whatever. The production was rich and sad, a sort of earthier, American answer to Stereolab, but with a hint of the earnest mawkishness of the whimper-core twee emo-pop I'd been almost exclusively listening to for the preceding year or two. So where would I file those American Analog Set records?—in the college years, when each one landed like a perfect sonic salve, impossibly gorgeous in a way that lit up my world and redefined what I thought indie music could be and do, or now, when I passionately want to be able to take those records out for late night spins on my turntable, preferably with a modest pour of whiskey, but can't, because I sold them off years ago. The answer should be obvious—I can't file those records anywhere, because I don't own them anymore, and I don't have the resources or the will to spend a hundred-plus bucks each on the secondary market replacing them.

*

I bought those American Analog Set records in my early days collecting, the earliest days, really, when my approach to buying records was haphazard, sloppy even. I split my money between tracking down favorites I already owned on CD, picking up whatever new releases I was excited about, and buying records from bands at shows. This phase of my collecting lasted for a number of years. It was fun, but messy, and I ended up with shelves full of records I didn't remember buying (I somehow wound up with *two* The Casket Lottery LPs whose origins I couldn't recall), records I bought on a whim because I'd heard good buzz about a band only to be disappointed (sorry, Radio 4), and plenty of records pity purchased from touring bands playing poorly attended shows (doubly sorry, Love as Laughter) that I would never revisit, would forget I even had, then, upon finding them on my shelves promptly take to the record shop with a stack of trade-ins. Looking back, this period felt like a waste of time and money, and yes, in a way it was—but it also helped me refine my sensibilities as a collector, helped me learn how to curate the collection that I wanted, or *thought* I wanted to own (though I still make a point of buying *something* from any touring band I see, as the economics of the music industry have made this one of the few ways many artists can make meaningful money).

Through this phase in my collecting, I was slowly learning how to be a more efficient, focused collector, which is what I thought I was working toward: heading into my thirties, I wanted a meticulously curated collection that celebrated the histories of pop, rock, and jazz, a collection that was built around a core of the traditional canon, and focused on only the most *important*, the most *essential* albums. I started using RateYourMusic to make lists of the "best" albums for every year from 1955 to the present. Then I tried to acquire as many of those albums as I could find, while also buying new albums that I suspected would end up on my current year end list. I started trading and selling records from my collection, both to fund this new direction, and to weed out records I deemed unworthy, rationalizing that this would better focus my collection, would help make it the platonic ideal of what a record collection should be, would transform it into an archive of *important* records. That's when I sold my American Analog Set Records (the first three, anyway—thankfully I kept 2001's *Know By Heart* because I knew I'd always need "Punk as Fuck" in my life). I deemed them, among other albums I loved and sold around the same time, unworthy. If, in that period of time, when I was trying to build a very specific type of collection, I believed that an album was inessential or passé, I would sell it. I learned some hard lessons. At one point, I sold a chunk of my 90s albums on eBay—included with those American Analog Set LPs were a first pressing of Pearl Jam's *No Code*, one of the first records I ever bought, before I was even really collecting, an original copy of the Pumpkins' *Pisces Iscariot*, and countless others including excellent, but less beloved and/or influential albums by the likes of R.E.M., Robert Pollard, Yo La Tengo, Sonic Youth, and Ted Leo, basically, a bunch of shit I loved, or at least liked very much, and had no business selling off, all because I didn't think any of it was *essential*, as if those records were somehow holding my collection back or diluting it.

In retrospect, the problem, here, was obvious: I was taking my collection too seriously, trying to build something too grand, pretentious, even, and in the process was limiting my enjoyment of collecting. Everything was informed by lists and what I perceived to be important. That didn't mean I never scored an exciting or unexpected find while crate digging, but I was so focused on those lists that I severely limited opportunities to make those scores. I took lists to the record store and looked for those albums, and frequently *just* those albums. And by selling and trading albums I loved because I didn't think of them as *essential*, either within the context of an artist's body of work, or in the larger cultural conversation of what makes music *important*, I was effectively creating a collection that wasn't for me, that didn't feel like it was mine. Of course, none of this is to say that a record collection shouldn't be periodically pruned, trading pieces out to make room on the shelf, or to buy records a collector is more excited about. But that's not what I was doing—I was selling records only because they didn't fit the narrow, arrogant vision I wanted for my collection. None of those albums I sold will ever show up on any meaningful "best ever albums" lists, but I now understand that they were important to my collection, and those are the albums that make my collection mine, are even, perhaps, the true heart of my collection.

It took me a while to figure that out, though, and by 2015, I'd built an expansive collection covering key genres, and almost every album in the collection was considered *important* or *essential* by someone, but not necessarily me. My collection felt airless, lifeless—there were still plenty of records

I loved on my shelves, but there was nothing about the collection surprising to me, no overlooked, odd ball gems I'd forgotten I owned, only to discover when reaching for something else entirely. Collecting records was no longer fun. It wasn't like I was going to stop, though. I just needed a new outlook.

*

Through 2015 and 2016 I moved away from, but didn't completely abandon, my list-maker's approach to record collecting. I kept two lists, and two lists only—one was a list of recent releases I might be interested in buying, and the other was a list of albums I didn't already own from Paul Gambaccini's 1987 book *Critic's Choice: The Top 100 Rock 'n' Roll Albums of All Time.* For those unfamiliar with the book, Gambaccini polled a shitload of DJs, MTV VJs, BBC radio personalities, and other music industry types to build a solid list of what Boomers at the time considered the greatest albums ever made. Why this book? Because a business associate gifted it to my father back when it was new, and not long after, as I was starting to get into older rock music, I couldn't stop reading it—the book was foundational in my development as a music fan. Yes, the book's list was ridiculously flawed thanks to some completely unsurprising solipsistic Boomer bullshittery: it included almost every Beatles album, for instance, including *Beatles for Sale*—it wasn't great. That said, the book was the reason I sought out Stevie Wonder's classic run of 70s records, as well as *Pet Sounds, What's Going On*, Richard and Linda Thompson, Joni Mitchell; it was how I learned Springsteen had albums before *Born in the USA*; and it also laid the groundwork that would inform my eventual love of indie and punk, through the likes of The Velvet Underground, Big Star, Bowie, Costello, Gang of Four, Roxy Music, Patti Smith, and The Clash. I know, I know—another list, *great*. But this list was different, was smaller, and actually important to me, *personally*. It didn't hurt that I already owned all but six of the albums from the book when I made this list—Simon & Garfunkel's *Bridge Over Troubled Water*, surprisingly, along with Lionel Richie's *Can't Slow Down*, The Eagles' *Hotel California*, Huey Lewis and The News' *Sports*, Don Henley's *Building the Perfect Beast*, and The Band's *The Last Waltz*, which was missing from my collection only because it was hard to find a copy that wasn't beat to shit. Buying those six records felt exciting—*Bridge* and *Waltz* because they were excellent albums I should have owned anyway, and the other four not because I liked them, but because they were part of the book, and therefore part of my story as a music fan. More importantly, though, those other four albums became weird surprises in my collection. Records I stumble upon while looking for something else and throw on the turntable from time to time. Even if I still don't love those records—Richie's is sounding better all the time, though—I like having them in my collection as weird detours.

I continued the focused list approach soon after when Rockathon Records released a book featuring the covers of what were, at the time, all 100 of Robert Pollard's LP releases with Guided By Voices and his various other projects. I worked from the Pollard book as my main list, but so long as I kept resources in reserve in case a hard-to-find Pollard record became available, I got back even further into crate digging, stumbling onto exciting finds and taking risks on records that seemed interesting that I wasn't familiar with. The list provided gentle structure for my hobby, gave me something to focus on and work toward, but having that anchoring force allowed for and even encouraged more joyful and exciting acts of collecting—as long as I was working on the list, I was going to keep collecting, but it wasn't so burdensome as to weigh down every trip to the record shop. The tension produced between the list-driven structure and the more playful crate digging, that had been such a significant part of vinyl's initial allure in the first place, ushered in a fun new era of collecting for me. Record shopping was enjoyable again, surprising, even. I was more likely to follow whims of inspiration to unexpected places—when I stumbled upon an out of print 2008 Polyvinyl reissue of Ida's third album, for instance, I got excited about 90s slowcore, leading to acquiring albums by Bedhead and filling in some missing Karate albums (that I'd also sold a while back), which reminded me of The Secret Stars, who brought me back around to Ted Leo, from whose catalog I was missing *Living with the Living* and *The Brutalist Bricks*, which, for reasons not entirely clear to me, reinvigorated my interest in Elvis Costello, much of whose discography I already owned, but there were and remain gaps, and then Costello led me back to The Roots, via their collaboration and on, and on, and on. My collection stopped being about what I believed was important, and more about tracing the weird, erratic contours of my taste. It was no longer trying to represent music history, it was telling a story about me.

Right now, my collection, over 2,000 records strong, is a strange and wooly, yet oddly satisfying archive of genres and levels of import: Atom and His Package sits next to Autre Ne Veut, Willie Nelson sits next to Neon Indian, Sublime next to Jim Sullivan, Vince Staples next to Stars of the Lid, Flying Burrito Brothers next to Flying Lotus, Dave Matthews Band next to John Maus, Taylor Swift next to Swimsuit next to Sza. It's a strange collection, bizarre, built out of the push and pull between expected classics and my own whims, interests, obsessions—and I love it. I'm always adding to it, tending to it, enjoying it. The list I'm currently using to guide my shopping is comprised of records I regret having sold—of course those three American Analog Set records are at the top, followed closely by *Pisces Iscariot*, and a number of other records I shouldn't have sold but did, more than I'd care to admit. Though I'm more cautious and thoughtful about it than before, I still sell and trade-in records—like a beloved plant, it's important to prune a collection, to clear out the albums that don't mean anything and just take up space, and also to upgrade worn out albums, initially purchased past their prime, or worn out from too many plays on my own turntable. It's a labor of love, buying, selling, trading, cleaning, organizing—and not for any good reason other than I enjoy it. Some guests to our house, or my Discogs page, might scoff at my collection, might take issue with my lack of King Crimson and Genesis, might judge me for owning not one but two Counting Crows albums, or even because I own the 4-lp box-set edition of The Flaming Lips' *Zaireeka*—which is so conceptually impractical that I never have, and almost certainly never will listen to it, but that's cool, I own it because they're one of the great bands from Oklahoma, and I lived there for six years. My collection isn't for everyone, and that's ok, it's for me, and I know that the right guests will appreciate it, and those who do, they'll run their fingers along the spines and feel a story begin to emerge, *my story*, will see something interesting and surprising catch their eye, slide it off the shelf and ask if we can give it a spin.

On Training Your Instincts

DRESSAGE
Siân Griffiths

Dressage, from French dressage, from dresser "to train, drill," means every part and every muscle. It means consistency. It means grinding. You may have gotten into this sport for fun, but fun is a pigment mixed in the medium of work.

The thing about riding is that not all days are nice. Most days, in fact, it's too hot or too cold or too wet or too dry. For months, all you will feel of your hands is their ache, and you will wonder how you ever believed there was such a thing as being too hot. For months, your sweat will be a river running down your spine and your eyes burns and blur with sunscreen and salt, and you will wonder that you failed to appreciate the cold. It would be easy to stop, but then you would cease to be a rider. Accept that this feeling, this dissatisfaction, will be the only true constant, but know too that this will also allow a fuller delight when the day is sunny and calm.

The amount you do not know about the body you've inhabited your whole life will come as something of a shock. Proprioception will allow you to become simultaneously firm and forgiving, engaged and relaxed. You will discover muscles through their function: The tiny little C of muscle near the base of your scalpula locks your shoulder down and back, allowing your elbow to give. The crease of muscle along the outside of your pelvis creating the rearward slide of your leg. The particular bit of hamstring telegraphs directly to the horse's hind foot, and the muscle inside your thigh just above your knee asks him to bend and engage.

The line between brilliance and disaster is razor fine. At first, you won't see it. You'll only know you've crossed it when things fall apart, but in these moments, you begin to sense it, and though this sense will feel foreboding and uncomfortable, it must become the feeling for which you strive. Without boldness, there can be no brilliance.

The masters of the art achieve the appearance of ease. This appearance is only arrived at through difficulty, strain, ugliness, and repeated failure.

Others, knowing nothing about riding, will tell you that it's easy. They will say it must be nice to have a hobby in a tone that makes it clear that they think you are wasting your life. They will assume that the horse does the work, that you need exert no effort. They will hold the appearance of ease against you, not understanding the work it took to create it.

You will spend too much time at the barn. You will spend too much money, too much sweat. Those whom you love will feel this as abandonment because how could they not? When this erupts in the occasional jealous comment, forgive them, knowing that jealousy is born from a place of love. You will love them better for your time at the barn, but there are days they will need all of you. You will need to split yourself. Become more.

The ribbons are pretty. Satisfying. Encouraging. Remember the ribbons are not the point. The point is the work, the struggle.

Speed is the enemy of impulsion. Power = drive + restraint. The paradox of drive and restraint is the basis on which all true collection is built. The horse, fearing his own power, will experiment, releasing it through a shoulder or letting it trail out behind like the tail to his kite. Collecting the power, the rider, too, will often hesitate, suddenly aware of danger inherent in so much bottled, explosive strength, but this is not the moment for fear. Rather, the rider must transmit confidence, allowing the horse his terrible magnificence.

The goal of training is a communication so subtle that the rider disappears. The dialogue between horse and rider becomes so fluid and fluent that the rider's movements become invisible, even as the horse appears to dance. The ultimate culmination of this is expression, is beauty, is art.

Some days, you won't want to train. Some days, you will want a mindless hack or the exhilaration of jumping fence rails. Listen to these impulses. Remember play and the love of the horse. The moments that have nothing to do with training have everything to do with training. Dailiness matters, but so too does rest.

Communication is both the core and the impossibility underlying each move you make. You will never know the full scope of the horse's thoughts nor he yours, but you find feelings can be shared through action and gesture. These moments of recognition are both minute and expansive. Addicting. They will move you outside the narrow confines of your skin and into a larger, glorious space, even as you remain aware of all you cannot know. A universe, even as it pulls larger, is preparing its collapse. Remembering this allows humility, humanity, compassion.

There will be moments when you try a new move too soon and the result will be chaos, disengagement, inversion. There will be moments when you try a new move and everything comes together—a gliding half pass, a floating passage—and you will know that the glorious feeling of this moment was built on every moment of struggle that came before.

The greatest riders to ever grace a saddle will lie on their death beds saying only now do they know enough to begin to learn to ride well.

There is no mastery, no perfection. There is only the pursuit. Really, though, is there any other purpose to which one could reasonably devote a life?

ON THE ANCIENT ART OF DRIVING ON A MOUNTAIN ROAD

Kirsten Reneau

When it's a road you know, one that you can and almost have done with your eyes closed, then there's something in your body that just understands. It is unexplainable to the man sitting beside you, who is holding onto your hand and the car door, *just from instinct*, you know, just in case the car rolls.

But the car has never rolled on you before and it's certainly not going to today.

The curves of the road here, you explain, *are built into the mountain, not through it.* It's environmentally conscious. It respects the land. You don't know if those reasons are true, but they feel like they should be. You don't like driving with people who don't live and travel regularly between the two towns. They don't do it *right*.

Right is unexplainable, again, but when you know it, you know it.

Back to the point.

When you are driving that long, one-way road (40 minutes between towns according to Google Maps, 36 minutes according to you) that connects your hometown to the next city over, the motions are rooted in your gut. Why do you slow down exactly this far from the curve? Why speed up here, in the road's swollen belly where three white crosses stand from someone who did not know the road like you did? How do you know in the back of your mind where the long stretches need to be, and where there will be a snake? There are no lessons you can give to outsiders. This is simply how to do it correctly.

You drive with one hand and one foot up between the window and the curve of your fingers that dance up and down the side of the wheel as you sway back and forth to the curve of the road. The music on the radio won't matter. You will be able to roll down the window and note how the wind sounds different depending on the angle of the mountain in relation to the speed of the car and in this way, you will feel so deeply in tune to what you are doing that nothing else will matter. The air will smell clean and it will seem like the entire earth is green.

This, you will explain again, *is an art,* and no one will understand how or why but you will know it to be true.

Of course, sometimes you must drive other roads, even ones from your hometown that you don't know as well. You must return to having two hands on the wheel, both feet down near the pedals. Google Maps will give you mile-by-mile updates. You will be told where to turn and slow down. But you will roll the windows down and turn up the radio.

Soon, this too will become known to you, as traceable on a map as the veins on your wrist.

HOW TO DELIVER
OTHER PEOPLE'S MAIL

Shane Kowalski

One of the first things they tell you at Carrier Academy is that—regarding the driving of mail trucks—people *will want* to drive their cars into you. The instructor says, "People think because we're government, they can get into an accident with one of our trucks and they'll get money. This is not the case." Everybody in the room seems to be asleep. The instructor goes on: so it is very important to stay vigilant, drive good, and make sure nobody drives their car into you. Then they show us a video about the importance of wearing a seatbelt where four people in a car, not wearing seatbelts, collide slow-mo into each other like in a pinball machine. Each person cracks their skull against each of the other peoples' skulls at least once. The sound effect they use for the skull-cracking sound sounds like it cost a lot.

But eventually, you come to find out, nobody is looking to drive their car into you. Everybody seems to just go about their business.

Casing mail involves taking already in-order mail (this includes first-class letters, third-class mail, and flats) and putting it into the correct slot in the case until all the mail is in the case. When all the mail is in the case, it looks like a bookcase for all the junk mail that you might accumulate in drawers in your house, only now it's vertical. You must make sure you account for forwards and holds on mail, too. They go in different slots. If you are delivering to an elderly facility or community, you must make sure every hardship gets delivered. This means bundling the mail off to the side and taking it directly to the door. Only after this is complete can you then "pull down." Pulling down involves taking all the mail you just put in the case and putting it back into the trays they came in. Now the mail is ordered! Now it can be "taken to the street." Sometimes casing the mail makes you feel like you want to die. Like there's a clock ticking inside you and every minute it gets closer to some arbitrary and unknowable hour, you feel like a hand bursting from a grave, only the grave keeps getting deeper, and you just keep bursting through more dirt.

Other times, casing the mail is very easy. When there is hardly any mail to case or when there are hardly any packages to put in order. Then you just look forward to taking it all to the street. Driving around the neighborhoods. Waving back at people waving at you. And then you're home by 3pm. There's still day left. You've delivered 400 - 500 people's mail and there's still time in the day left to do whatever you like to do. You think you could do this every day for the rest of your life.

The first time you deliver an entire route yourself, you will probably cry. You will probably choke back tears while delivering mail. You will probably feel like you can't distinguish between sweat and tears by the end of it all.

"Follow the mail" is a common piece of advice for new carriers. If you get lost out there—and you will probably get lost—just start "following the mail." Which means what exactly? It means you look at the address of the next piece of mail and you find the corresponding mailbox on the street. But by this time, you'll have taken the wrong turn, or several wrong turns, or passed several mailboxes that didn't seem like they belonged to anybody living. So, when you finally start "following the mail," you have no fucking clue where or how or what to follow. You will pass by the same house, back and forth, at least three or four times—you'll begin to wonder if the people inside are getting suspicious (because for all the trust people place in their mailman, they also are suspicious when the mail truck keeps flinging by). What do you do? You are so far out in the sticks, your phone's GPS is wonky or unwilling to work. You want to drive to a secluded side of road and just abandon the truck. Walk into the cornfield and disappear. Maybe appear back in life as someone's cob of corn at a holiday dinner. But you can't do this. You must deliver the rest of the mail. By the time you are done, it is 8pm, it is dark, and you smell like gasoline and paper. You think: Have I gone mad?

There was a former marine who joined the post office. He was very tall, very in-shape, looked almost like he could kill anything he wanted to without impunity. This is who we want delivering mail, one supervisor said. Another said: This man is built to carry mail. He has discipline.

First day on the job, the marine never returned. They tracked his scanner to a collection box, where he had left his bag of mail with a note that said: "Sorry, I can't do this. My feet hurt."

Finally, one summer, an old woman in a BMW is seemingly, very slowly, driving right into my mail truck. *Is she going to drive right into my truck?* I think. *Is it finally going to happen?* I am as far off to the side as I can be on this rural road in Pennsylvania. She doesn't hit me but very slowly scrapes the left side of the mail truck. It sounds like it does in the movies. I watch as the car pulls of the side of the road behind me and begins turning around. It takes forever for the car to maneuver this, and so I stand next to the mail truck. There seems, miraculously, to be no scratches or scrapes—at least not any new ones. Eventually the BMW drives back. The old woman driving is a hunched-over, squirrel of a person, with bulging, darting eyes, and a neck strangled by a pearl necklace. I immediately notice the utter state of disrepair the BMW is in. Scrapes, dents, scratches…this car is quietly wrecked. The old woman behind the wheel asks if I'm okay as she simultaneously begins driving away, unconcerned with a response. The car gains speed until it's just a blur down the street. I'm okay, I say. I think nobody will ever know about this. Nobody who opens their mail today will ever know what it took to put it in their hands.

ADVENTURES IN BIRD (MIS)IDENTIFICATION
Ruth Joffre

I. Pigeon guillemot

A shorebird of family Alcidae, also called an alcid or auk, the pigeon guillemot lives, breeds, and hunts on the shores of the North Pacific. Mature breeding adults are black from beak to butt, with the exception of a small patch of white on its wings bisected by another line of black feathers. Its webbed feet are a deep blood orange. In photographs, its open mouth is this same shocking color, as if it has coated its entire mouth in fish blood. A vampire bird, not at all like the pigeons on the sidewalks of Seattle, with their iridescent feathers and ridiculous little waddle. (Rock pigeons, in fact, are part of a different family, Columbidae, along with their less reviled cousins, doves.)

We spot this pigeon guillemot bobbing in the water off of a spit in Homer, Alaska. That knifelike curve of rock and road where Alaska Route 1 ends and the beach looks out over Kachemak Bay. That is, quite literally, the end of the road, the westernmost point of the Alaskan road system and the farthest you can get in the U.S. without a boat, plane, or snowmachine. We're here for a work trip, a combination teambuilding excursion and planning exercise to prepare for the next year. Of what, I cannot tell you. My NDA precludes me from explaining who my clients are, what they do in

Alaska, what I do for them. I cannot tell you their names, but I can say: they aren't just clients. Of everyone I'm paid to work with, they are the ones I like best, the ones who picked me and my girlfriend up at the airport in Anchorage and drove us to the Kenai Peninsula, pausing every sixty or so miles so we could snap photos of glaciers and mountains—the ones, I should say, who paid for this work trip, expensed it all away, a line item in their budget.

Before embarking on this trip, my girlfriend, a consummate outdoorswoman, took me to REI so I could get proper gear for Alaska in mid-September: a fleece, a windbreaker, some rain pants I've forgotten to pack. Even so, it's bitter cold on the spit, a fierce wind ripping the hood of my jacket clean off my head and chilling me to the bone. My shoulders ache from tensing against the winds and my jaw is freezing, my TMJ screaming at me to warm up, but I can't say, "Let's go"—not in this situation. My client is enthralled. Almost as soon as we stepped onto that rocky beach, an ink black pelagic cormorant flew past us, and then another and another. My girlfriend and I carefully pick a path over the rocks and find twin seashells on the beach, like miniature conches with their curves sliced off so that only the central spiral and a thin lobe of shell remain. When held side by side, the shells form a heart. We pocket them as keepsakes.

Everything around us is wondrous: the glacial gray of the waters, the gelatinous orange stripes of a beached jellyfish, the towering peaks of Kachemak Bay State Park, mere miles across the water (close enough so that it feels like we could swim to them and back, though our lungs would seize the moment we slipped into the not-quite freezing water). A black-legged kittiwake flies down to shore and lands beside us, not six feet away, unbothered by our surprise or the many photographs we take with our iPhones. I send one to my best friend, a real birder, who loses her shit at the fact that I am here, in Alaska, seeing birds she may never see in her lifetime. It hits me then: how rare it is to encounter certain birds, what a privilege it is to be in the right place at the right time. Most movies and television shows don't bother with showing the right birds for the region. Every song is available in post-production, so all birds could be anywhere. The Eastern screech owl in sunny California. A red-bellied woodpecker in the Pacific Northwest. In movies, the call of a bald eagle is usually replaced with the call of a red-tailed hawk. Bald eagles, it turns out, sound like strange, high-pitched seagulls, some of their chirps recalling bad sci-fi sound effects. Not majestic at all.

When I spot a black bird bobbing and diving off the shore, something clicks inside me: the desire to know, to be able to call each thing by its right name—or, at least, one of the names we humans have given it with all our myriad languages. Pigeon guillemot. I know its behavior before I know its name and its family, before even I learn the word alcid. In this moment, it is just a small black bird rocking on the waves, diving for long minutes in search of food. My client theorizes: a loon? Another diving bird, capable of staying under for up to six minutes, he says, reading from an app for bird identification: Merlin. I downloaded it months ago but have not used it. I open it up now, grateful for one bar so I can update my bird packs, add the one for Alaska.

For the first time, I attempt to identify a bird through the app. It asks: what size was the bird? Not too big, a bit larger than a robin but certainly smaller than a crow. Black and swimming. The first option that comes up is the marbled murrelet, a small shorebird, also black, also pictured bobbing on the waves—but what about the common murre? Or the pigeon guillemot? How do you tell the difference? Bill shape, my client says, then behavior, then color—though color (as another birder informs me, much later) can often lie. We try to focus on the bill, peering through his binoculars, passing them back and forth so we each get a turn; but this bird is moving, searching for fish, and by the time we center it in our sights it's already diving, disappearing. Its elusiveness makes it all the more intriguing. Half an hour passes and all I can see is a wing: black but with a white blotch marred by another, darker blotch. Chromatic aberration makes it look reddish, rust colored, but it might be black. I'm almost sure it's black.

Everyone but my client thinks, *pigeon guillemot*—has to be, but he demurs. It could be a cross of the black and the pigeon guillemot; then again, it could be something else entirely. Who can say? How do we know what we think we know? At this stage of the Anthropocene, in the second year of a pandemic, the brief window between mass vaccination and a new variant has filled us with a tentative hope: that the worst is over, that it is safe to go outside again—safe enough, even, to get on a plane and fly more than 1,400 miles to meet my clients in person for the first time, after two years of video calls. We tell ourselves the trip is worth it, believe that by masking up indoors and never once eating out we're minimizing the risk. We do not yet know what a gamble this is. How disinformation has gradually eroded our society, not over weeks or months but over decades, and now it's virtually impossible to save ourselves or our planet from the overlapping apocalypses of COVID, climate change, and capitalism.

In the end, I log the black/pigeon guillemot cross. It will not count as a sighting of either species.

II. Great horned owl

A "true owl" of family Strigidae, as distinguished from barn owl family Tytonidae by their round faces, arresting yellow eyes, and adorable little ear tufts, which heart-faced barn owls lack. Great horneds are not actually the largest owls (that distinction belongs to a type of eagle owl known as Blakiston's fish owl, which has a wingspan of up to six and a half feet, about a foot wider than I am tall), but the great horned is in many respects the quintessential owl—the one people picture when they think "owl." Its enormous eyes evolved to be cylindrical in shape, similar to manmade telephoto lenses, and provide the great horned with impeccable night vision, as well as the ability to spot prey at vast distances. In flight, the serrated edge and trailing fringe of its feathers allow it to glide silently through the night air and snap up unsuspecting prey. Its sharp talons can exert up to five hundred pounds of pressure per square inch—far more than a mere human hand and more than enough to snap a rodent's neck.

I hear my first great horned owl on a chilly October night, about a month after our trip to Alaska. My girlfriend and I huddle around a crackling orange campfire in Wallace Falls State Park, about one hour from Seattle, where we lived at the time. A friend of hers was unable to use the cabin she booked because she had a last-minute conflict arise. It was too late to cancel, so she gifted us this reservation, and we drove up last-minute in the silver Subaru my girlfriend bought from the same friend earlier that year. In our hiking boots and flannel, we were living our gay fantasy, and when we hiked up to Middle Falls, the second (and best) vantagepoint on the trail, the waterfall seemed to acknowledge us by casting a glorious, shimmering rainbow. Nature is not subtle.

Nor is it comfortable. Our cabin, at least, is heated, the sad, flat mattress shelled in a material like the green cover of a barstool, but outside it is chilly and our stomachs rumble. We have not really brought enough food, and my body's screaming for one thing: chocolate. Every month, when my menstrual cycle hits and it feels like an iron rod has impaled my lower back, I want nothing more than to curl up with a hot water bottle and drink chocolate milkshakes on tap. My cramps weren't always this painful. Anecdotal evidence suggests the COVID-19 vaccines intensified them, but it could also be that I walk a lot less than I used to and my muscles are mad at me. I never stretch. I always forget how much exercise really does make me feel better, which is why, when this friend offered us the cabin, I decided to push through the discomfort and go for a hike anyway. Luckily, the ibuprofen kept the cramps at bay most of the day.

Now, it's late and I'm shivering in front of the campfire while we wait for the wood to burn itself out. I hear it then: the great horned owl—its deep, throaty call, peaking on the third hoot and then falling with the final two. Distinctive. Memorable. It's my first time hearing it. I open the app for help with an ID, listen to different owl calls to understand differences in pitch, intonation. Barred owls are known for their call, which sounds like a question: "Who cooks for you?" A short-eared owl, listed as uncommon in this area, has one call that sounds like a cat objecting to a hand on its belly. Another of its calls sounds like the scream of a warrior psyched up for battle. According to eBird, an app birders use to track species they have identified, a northern pygmy owl and western screech owl have also been found in Wallace Falls State Park, but the entry for the latter dates all the way back to 1996 and may only be an audio ID.

Amongst birders, audio IDs can be a topic of debate. Are they good enough? Can you be sure? A lot of birds have similar calls, and it's easy to misidentify bird songs. Even the Merlin app makes mistakes, once confusing the distant laugh of a young boy hiking with his mother for the call of a great horned. Still: it's a unique sound (unlike the calls of most other owls in this area) and could only be mistaken for one other bird, the barred owl, whose call is four beats long. Not five. In the dark, I try to parse what I heard, to recreate the sound in my throat—the deep, ominous timbre of a bird of prey capable of striking without sound. I imagine it gliding through the cool night air up above, hearing my attempts to mimic its call. Dismissing me as a poser, a human. I mean nothing to this bird, except that my species is destroying its habitat. Our shared planet. For now, the great horned is not endangered and its conservation status is low concern, but bigger and stronger owls have gone extinct before. Blakiston's fish owl populations have dwindled to an estimated 1,000 – 1,900 specimens in total. It may well go extinct before I ever get a chance to see it.

In the end, I decide to log the great horned owl with just the audio ID.

As of this writing, eBird still lists it as the latest logged instance of the bird in Wallace Falls State Park.

III. Tundra swan

A whistling swan first described in written English by colonizers Meriwether Lewis and William Clark near the end of their journey, below the place where the Columbia River narrows through a curve before cutting through its namesake gorge. A journal entry dates the encounter to March of 1806, at a time of year when great flocks of swans are migrating back north to breed in the Arctic tundra, which gives this species (*Cygnus columbianus*) its common name. By sight, tundra swans are notoriously difficult to distinguish from their more common cousins, trumpeter swans. A tiny patch of yellow or orange on the more rounded beak differentiates this somewhat smaller species from its large relative. Lewis and Clark noted a difference in the calls: the trumpeter swan honks, its call like twin trumpets tooting back and forth at each other, whereas tundra swans give single, hitch-pitched bugles, like a brassy whistle.

It's this bugling call I hear as I pick my way through the twilit mud of the Skagit Bay estuary one chilly February evening when the last rays of sun turn the sky first orange, then pink, then finally a tender shade of purple, like a patch of barely bruised skin. My girlfriend walks up ahead, awash in the splendor of the marsh and the sunset disappearing on the horizon even as her nose and ears start to freeze. We do this every Saturday: a walk, an adventure—anything to get us up and out in this cold, dreary place, where the sun sets around 5pm and is almost always obscured by clouds. Before the pandemic, when I actually went into the office, I would leave in the dark and return in the dark, my days bookended by a pitch black sky. Working from home, the bookends disappear, and life becomes defined by blankets, by candles, by soup in its many variations. We must go out or risk wilting into the comforter, like plants deprived of sun.

On our drive to the estuary, we spotted trumpeter swans—a handful off the highway, a couple on the corner—but nothing like the hundreds will we see in April, when we return to watch the huge flocks gather in the muddy fields of the Skagit Flats (an important breeding ground for migratory birds). Some 60,000 snow geese return here each spring, the flocks so dense and thick the ground looks like it is covered in a sheet of ice and snow. Driving up the access road, we spotted three or four of them, along with several swans— trumpeters, we assumed, because they're more common in this area and because we have grown used to seeing them since first spotting them in Alaska in September. We think we know their elegant, curved neck. Their feathery white butts lifting in the air whenever their heads dip into the water to dig up weeds. Who knew? We didn't expect to find tundra swans. We weren't sure what we would find.

When we arrived at this wildlife management area, a northern harrier was pecking at the muck in reeds, not far from our car, and the Merlin app quickly identified its shrill call. I waited, hoping it would take flight, and was rewarded for this patience by the sight of it soaring out within ten feet of us, clearly identifiable by the trademark white stripe across the back of its tail. I thrilled at this sighting, not just because it was a new bird but because it brought my life list to ninety-eight. Just two away from one hundred—extremely doable, I thought, for one walk. When I first got serious about birding, I would regularly get four or five new birds on each outing, just because there was so much I hadn't seen yet. On one walk, I got a great blue heron, spotted towhee, American coot, and red-winged blackbird—all species I have seen many times since. Almost every time I go out, I recognize the bright white head and dark blue stripes over the eyes of the great blue heron, now a familiar friend.

As I walk through the reeds I wonder what bird #100 will be. An owl, maybe? Or another kind of raptor? I keep scanning the sky, watching the stars wink to life and the moon cut its pale crescent shape in the darkening sky. Everything looks soft, fuzzy, like the whole world has been draped in gauze. In the distance, a white object out of range of my binoculars looks alternately like a stump or a barn owl or a ghost come to haunt me in my waking moments. No birds sing around me. It's getting late, I realize, late enough for nocturnal predators to start hunting and too late to be losing my girlfriend in the encroaching gloom. I call to her from the other side of a gully she jumped. In the distance, her voice is bright, elated—soon to be drowned out by the loud honks of a gaggle of Canada geese flying overhead; and then, in their wake, another, quieter sound: a whistle, a bugle. Three tundra swans in a tight V. I record them to be sure. To have some proof of my 99th bird.

There are 11,162 known species of birds in the world today. Who knows how many there will be by the time I die?

On Trusting the Process

A GARDEN IS A LOVE SONG
Abby Harding

When I was a child, I longed for a perfect, magical garden. This garden could either come with fairies hiding among the roses or with a hidden entrance only I knew about–I wasn't picky. What really mattered to me was the way I believed I'd *feel* in such a garden: full of wonder, my heart bursting with the bittersweet perfection of the moment. *Barber's Adagio*, but make it flowers.

No matter how many times I asked, though, my mother always had the same response: if you want a garden, you're going to have to make it yourself. This was usually enough to make me give up with a few dirty looks and wordless grumbles, but occasionally I would actually try to bring my vision to life. Mostly, this involved walking around the yard, trying to picture where a garden could go, then half-heartedly pulling a couple weeds or arranging bricks into some semblance of bed edging.

Every time, I wound up sorely disappointed by my (lack of) results, and I'd give up before I'd really even begun. If I couldn't create the lush, blousy garden of my dreams in a few hours, then it wasn't worth it.

Of course, the real problem was that I didn't know what I was doing or how to learn, and I didn't have the patience to coax a garden into being, or even an appreciation for the process. I wanted to enjoy the reward and skip the work part, thank you very much.

I also felt that gardening should come naturally to me, because there was family precedent: my grandmother was a very knowledgeable gardener. When she retired from teaching high school science at the end of the 80s, she pivoted and dove headlong into her dream job of growing herbs and vegetables on the family land and sharing her products and knowledge with the community. She ran her farm for over 25 years and became a known expert in our area on how to cultivate culinary herbs in particular. I had inherited her love of cats and cross-stitch, I reasoned, so why didn't gardening come easily to me?

Finally, when I was fresh from high school (circa 2005), I began working on the farm during my summers, and my passion for the *idea* of gardening began to grow legs and become a passion for the *process* of gardening. I began to learn how to learn.

Grandma was the one who taught me to plant a tomato up to its first true leaves, that you have to start cilantro from seed every few weeks if you want it all summer, and which plants (like cucumbers and pumpkins) are better off being seeded directly into the fields and not started in the greenhouse. I finally had the beginnings of knowledge, and, even better, I had someone to go to with questions or who could correct me when I didn't know what I was doing.

Even with all my new knowledge, though, my first independent gardening attempts were...tepid. I didn't set a budget for it, I didn't have a real plan, and, more importantly, I hadn't really *committed* to being a gardener. I was still more in love with the image of being a gardener than the actual work of gardening. I hated the fact that most gardens take years to become established, and that even with all the head knowledge in place, I still had to spend countless hours on my knees with my hands in the dirt, sweat trickling down the back of my tee shirt. It wasn't until my family bought our first house that I began to invest myself in the work, to act like a gardener instead of just dreaming about it.

I spent hours digging up plants that were in the wrong spots (too tall, too much sun, not enough sun) and relocating them somewhere better. I devoured gardening books, discovering what I liked and what I didn't and stealing ideas to use in my own space. I decided I wanted to put an herb garden in a bed the previous homeowner had mulched with gravel, and I spent an entire week sifting rocks out of the dirt with a homemade sieve.

And don't get me started on the weeds. So. Many. Weeds.

That first year, I focused on the bones, the underlying shape of the garden. It looked good–far better than it had–but it was a little thin. There were times I was discouraged with how long it took to see any real progress. I was still focusing on the product, and not enough on the process. But slowly, ever so slowly, my yard began to look more like that dreamy oasis I'd pictured as a kid. Finally, there was an evening where I sat on the porch, breathing the summer air and listening to the crickets, where I looked around and thought, "It's almost perfect."

Of course, we moved a few months later, and I had to start the process all over again.

But I wasn't starting from scratch. This most recent garden has gone the most smoothly of any garden to date. I know so much more about planning now, how to sketch out the shape of garden beds and how to pick plantings that work together visually, thinking about their size, color, and texture. I make far fewer missteps than I used to.

I'm still learning–I can't stop, really. I have always loved botanical gardens, but since I began gardening myself, my appreciation for a well thought-out garden space has grown exponentially. It turns out that one of the best teachers is someone else's successful garden. With practice, I've learned how to identify plants and parse out what makes a garden work, and now it comes automatically: "Oh, I like how they layered those hostas" or "that's a good use of color blocking" or "I want to build a succulent wall!"

Sometimes, I still catch myself growing impatient, longing for perfection, and I have to remind myself that the process itself has to be reward enough. Sure, there are seasons when you can barely keep up with the production, when the summer days are long, the night air redolent with the scent of squash vines, and lightning bugs glint in the dusk. But not most of the time. In my climate, there is a one to two month window (at best) where the garden is at its peak. The rest of the year, the plants are small, the work is long, and the yard might not look like much—or it's covered in snow and not growing anything at all. If all I wanted was a tomato, the grocery store or the farmers market would have them for far less expense and hassle. I have to want more than the produce. I have to want the process, the feeling of my hands in the dirt and my nose full of a smell you can't describe without the word "earthy."

Don't get me wrong, harvest time is sweet. Sitting on the porch in the glow of evening, watching bees and hummingbirds sip from my flowers while I eat juicy cherry tomatoes straight from the vine, is euphoric. As I drink in the wild beauty of my garden, I become that little girl again, convinced I just saw a fairy darting behind a pumpkin leaf. In those fleeting, near-perfect moments, I hear music.

HEART, SOUL & DROPS OF BLOOD
Ashleigh Catibog-Abraham

It starts with a heartbeat. A tiny flicker on the ultrasound screen. Everything that needs to be done isn't neatly wrapped in a package with a bow on top. The vitamins. The food. The appointments. Then comes the waiting. Weeks and months of waiting. There is the illusion that there is time to spare. Life forms so slowly and so quickly simultaneously. At halfway, you feel the smallest flutters. Which turn into distinct kicks. Suddenly there is no more room to grow. The plug is pulled, the water begins to drain. The pain is immeasurable, so intense you can't see straight. But you only have one thought in mind. Pushing through seems like nothing compared to what's waiting for you at the end. A wave comes. And you meet the person you have been living with for almost a year. Finally, you get to hold your creation in your arms.

THOUSANDS OF HALF-STITCHES
Katharine Coldiron

I cross-stitch. The hyphen denotes a type of embroidery: two brief stitches cross each other in the shape of an X. Thousands of X shapes fill a canvas of special fabric, called aida (no relation, as far as I know, to the opera *Aida*, about an eponymous princess), which is threads woven into a miniature pegboard with premade holes at perfectly regular intervals, through which my needle draws thread, one half-stitch at a time.

The thread I use to cross-stitch is a specific type called embroidery floss, largely made of satinized cotton. The company that makes the floss, DMC, produces more than 500 shades, as distinct and as near each other as the colors of a dawn sky. Each color has a number. Websites exist that use mathematical algorithms to match shades, in case you can't get 3325 but already have 800 in your stash. "Stash" is a term for a crafter's store of materials, whether skeins of yarn (knitters) or boxes of beads (jewelry-makers). My stash of DMC colors numbers 329 bobbins. I recently spent $350 on a custom wooden chest to store them, in drawers, in numerical order. It's important to me that my stash be very tidy and well-kept.

I have made dozens of projects over about 20 years; in preparing this essay, I tried to count them all but could not. The most meaningful project I've ever made is one of the earliest I still have: a 16" x 13" portrait of the *Titanic* passing through the North Atlantic, tiny crossed stars in yellow fixed in an aida sky of navy blue. I made this during the worst period of my life, and it hangs on a wall I see every day to remind me what it is to finish something difficult.

Cross-stitching involves, in essence, color-by-number with needle and thread. The charts indicate exactly how many stitches of each color should be made on a piece of aida of specific size and shape. The charts tell you everything practical you need to know about the project. They don't tell you how to keep going, or how good it's going to look, or how many hours it'll take—these are all mysteries that can only unfold in progress, once you've gathered the floss colors and cut the aida, when it's hard to turn back. All other details are laid out, though. You can calculate exactly how many stitches are in the pattern—only, then you must double it, because each is two stitches, \ and /.

When people look at my cross-stitch projects, they compliment me. They have used mostly visual words: beautiful, colorful, cute, lovely. The word "creative" has been said from time to time. I do not feel good about this word to describe my cross-stitch projects. It's stitch-by-number, I want to explain. I didn't design the pattern; I just followed the directions.

I have learned that a surprising number of people do not follow the directions.

Is cross-stitch a creative art? I feel safe enough saying that it *produces* objects of art, that, in the "create" sense we attribute to God or a pregnant body, it creates. But in the looser sense of the word, the one we attribute to Rothko or DiFranco, I'm unsure. I use almost no creative latitude when stitching. I've designed only two patterns, and for those I piggybacked on other work: a peacock from a book of patterns, a special alphabet from an online designer.

I think of cross-stitching as making Tollhouse cookies.

Anyone can follow the recipe, even if I mix the dough in my bowls and bake it in my oven. The stitches pass through my mind, heart, and fingers before appearing in a pleasing pattern on the fabric, but another person could very easily produce an indistinguishably identical result with her own mind, heart, and fingers.

I have no memory of how I came to this art form, if art form it is. I used to rely on kits, which come with the pattern, the canvas, a needle, and sufficient colors and lengths of floss to complete a design. Over time I used these less and less, the same way you might stop buying bottled sour mix and start making your own if you get deep enough into cocktail culture. I buy needles separately now, from a woman who invented a spiral-eye needle that brilliantly avoids threading.

Like a lot of fiber arts, cross-stitching is the same thing over and over for however long it takes to be done. The variations in method seem minor in the wide view of the craft, but become more significant as you get closer. (Similarly, most projects don't make sense when you're looking at them from inches away, as you must in in order to make them. When finished, everything changes as distance and perspective do.)

Projects with huge swaths of single colors can be tedious, but filling in all that space is like Sharpie-ing a whole piece of paper until it's completely black: satisfaction unequaled. Projects with a lot of fiddly little color changes in a limited space can be frustrating, even daunting, but the chaos of those colors renders a whole different satisfaction upon zooming out.

The weirdest way of all is gradient work, where a dozen small variations of color approximate photorealism. The color combinations are totally illogical, so, in the stitching, you must rely on counting squares to follow the pattern, as you cannot recognize a greater overall purpose to each stitch. That is: in stitching a flower rendered in the 8-bit visual language cross-stitch forces upon objects, you can lean back and see where petals, stem, stigma, leaf go in the design, what colors will probably go where. But gradient patterns make no sense until they're fully finished. Even when I had less than a dozen stitches to go on a gradient pattern of a face, I had no idea how those stitches would make the finished product look better. I had to trust the pattern rather than my own eyes.

Again, though, a pattern with riotous color or gradient confusion calls for less pure stamina than a pattern of huge color blocks. That *Titanic* stitch required inches upon inches of crossed black, to form the bow, belly, and stern of the great doomed vessel. Days, weeks, I stitched only black. DMC 310. Every stitcher knows this number. One community has even designed a cryptid pattern around DMC 310. We all need it for nearly any design—if not for a shadow or a shade, for backstitch.

Backstitch is the outline, the boundary. It runs between the pink flesh of a Caucasian face (225) and the bright sky behind her (809). It forms walls and floors and legs and hair, messages, mouths; the suggestion of anything around which a line can be drawn. Backstitch is a necessary finishing step for a majority of cross-stitch projects, and I hate doing it. I hate it for three reasons, only two of which I understand.

I'm not an embroiderer; I'm a *cross-stitcher*. I stitch in Xs. Asking me to draw lines across my own handiwork just to demarcate one thing from another asks me to disparage both the pattern and the viewer of my work. You must force a drawn beak on that bird, a drawn edge on this window? The pattern could not have been designed to show these elements with color alone? The viewer cannot be asked to imagine these dimensions herself?

Beyond the philosophical, I hate backstitch because it's less methodical and much easier to mess up. Undoing and re-doing backstitch is harder (if shorter) than undoing and re-doing cross-stitch. Something about it, as a skill, extends beyond following directions. Follow the pattern perfectly and your backstitch still might look wonky if your hands can't perform it right. A fun challenge for plenty of crafters; a swamp of uncertainty for me.

(At some point in the 2010s I simply stopped doing French knots. These are dots formed by a specific floss trick/configuration, good for stars and pupils and other small round elements in a pattern. I tried again and again and could not get the hang of them, so I refuse to do them at all, substituting a tiny quarter-stitched X in most cases.)

Backstitch is the finishing step, as I said, and this could explain the inexplicable part of my dislike for it. I don't like finishing things. I like *doing* things. I like the goal inherent in an unfinished thing. Once it is finished, what will happen to it? This object I have handled for weeks or months, that I made into art from a blank canvas, a needle, and floss—now it goes into the dormant state of *finished*. No longer handled, no longer full of potential; shelved or rolled or hung up, over. My active control over it has lapsed, and it is just another completed thing.

The only facet of cross-stitching I truly don't like, that I find uncomfortable instead of just personally irritating (fray-prone specialty threads, patterns with beading), is how it figures in to the history of fiber arts. Knitting is and always has been a practical craft, one which makes useful objects. Repaired objects, warming objects, protective objects. Cross-stitching and embroidering make objects only for seeing, rarely for touching, and never for practical use. Rich women cross-stitched, in centuries past. Poor women knitted. Idle women with no practical skills could cross-stitch; women with resilience and determination could knit.

Objects made only for seeing have their own species of value, but it's not use value. Let me be clear. We require art to survive, but not in the same way we require food and clothing.

I stopped knitting many years ago out of impatience for how long it took to see progress. (I find I'm happy to finish *useful* things—cooking meals, making paper, building furniture, these don't trigger my reluctance to finish.) Every row adds to the garment, but unless you make small garments or knit very fast, seeing those additions, distinguishing them from the whole week's progress, is difficult, even impossible in some patterns. Sweaters take so long that I'd stretch them when holding them up to myself, visually lying about how many more rows it would take to cover my body, so I'd be done faster. I wound up making crop-top sweaters with three-quarter sleeves, unwearable because they didn't warm, didn't protect.

By contrast, a cross-stitch project looks different every single day. The progress is obvious after only a few minutes' work. The aida begins blank, but every stitch makes it one square less blank. One small bit of proof at a time that I exist, that I was here, that I made a mark. I produce something every time I pick up the needle: every half-stitch is visual confirmation that I am a creator. The scale, the tedium, the inspiration, the mistakes don't matter.

You must have patience to cross-stitch. You must seek repetition. You must be willing to buy tiny skeins of floss by the dozens at 63¢ a pop. You must have access to uninterrupted solitary time, or you must be able to explain to others that you are listening *while* you stitch, that it soothes you to stitch while you listen, that a part of you listens *better* when your hands are occupied. (You may remember the feeling of chain-smoking while you talked to someone all night, well into the wee hours, and how your hands flicking ash and cupping a flame could not be parted in your memory from the connection you felt, from the depth of conversation.) You must place trust in Etsy. You must have no quarrel with producing something that has no use value, only aesthetic value. You *must follow the directions.*

I put my initials and the date (in backstitch) on every project I finish. In this way I show that it was *me* who made this, me specifically, in that month, in that year. I filled up that canvas with the work of my hands. I was here. I am here.

On Noticing

SILENT TREATMENT
Hattie Hayes

It was my first working interview, and I asked the girl at the front desk why she was leaving. "I got my dream job," she said, "at an organic dog food company." I asked what she would be doing there, and she said, "Working at the front desk."

I didn't dream of being a receptionist at a dog food company, but I also didn't dream of being a receptionist at a global financial firm, which was what I was, after my working interview became a training session midway through. The outgoing incumbent had worked at the financial firm for a number of years, despite being twenty-three, a full two years younger than I was at the time. Her main priority was answering the telephone, she told me, but sometimes she also put client meetings on the calendar, or did light filing around the office. Within a day of my interview, I had a 9 to 5. I was the girl at the front desk.

In the seven months I held that job, the phone rang no more than twenty times. I did light filing around the office, or put client meetings on the calendar. Every morning, I picked up the *New York Times* from the basket outside the office doors, and placed it on the foyer table, throwing away the previous day's edition. Twice a month I printed and spiral-bound client presentations, which ranged between 15 and 96 pages, depending on the size of the portfolio. In the six weeks leading up to Christmas, I hand-folded, hand-stuffed, and hand-labeled approximately 1,890 holiday cards (1,450 domestic, 440 international). And on Friday nights, I cleaned the kitchen.

There were three other women in that office, two executives and an associate, and none of them ever learned my name. Lily, who approved my timesheets and sent them to the temp agency every week, called me Hallie. Caroline and Janhavi just called me "the girl." Even before I walked out, this didn't offend me one bit. It was comforting to know if I wanted to leave their lives forever, they would be eager to forget. They clearly didn't care about me, but I didn't mind that either. They disliked one another so much that I was happier unnoticed.

This is the part I didn't like: I was not allowed to do anything. My most important duty was answering the phone, but no one called. I was not permitted to use the computer, except to add meetings to the calendar, or print presentations. Filing took up an hour of my time each week, but when I stood at the filing cabinets, Lily and Caroline would sigh and glare at me. I tried to get it done before or after they were in the office. I was not allowed to read (it would look unprofessional if someone walked in), or use the internet (it would look unprofessional if someone walked in). I learned not to write in my notebook while at the front desk, because Janhavi would ask questions about "what I was working on" if she suspected it was a project for someone else.

The girl who trained me did not give any indication that my days at the investment company would be spent in complete silence, but on especially tense days, none of the other staff would speak at all, even to me. During my shifts, I would sit, quietly, and listen, quietly, to the corporate quiet of the rooms and the building. We were on the 24th floor in midtown. Packages were received by a concierge downstairs, who left them wordlessly in the basket with the *New York Times*, but every now and then we got visitors, all men. The IT guy who came to check the servers. The IT guy who came to check the printer. The secure shredding services guy who came to move the papers from our locked trash can to his locked trash can. Once or twice, a guy from the real estate office across the hall, who would ask Lily to notarize documents.

My jobs before this one had all been journalism jobs, which required me to put words on paper and then talk to other humans to collect more words. I was a chute, now I was a vessel. This was new to me. I was not talking or listening. I had never had silence in my life but I had never looked.

The first few weeks weren't as bad as you might think. I was not unhappy, but I was concerned I was doing something wrong. To fill my time, I allowed myself more performance anxiety than is typical for me. Before she left, the original girl assembled a manual with all of her knowledge, and once I had it memorized I went through every email template and filing index to make sure they matched. Some days, I tried to keep busy by cleaning out an old desk or organizing the supply drawers. Everyone in the office hated that.

There was never even any paperwork or clutter on my desk. I memorized its surface, the nicks and dings, an amateur traveler wringing meaning from stars. There were two types of pens in the office and I formed opinions. Caroline and I preferred the Pilot Precise V5 Rollerballs, and when we ordered supplies, I would get a multi-pack of colors and keep the greens for myself. Paper Mate InkJoy Gels came in an array of colors too, but we went through the blue and black ones so quickly I never added other colors to the order or felt bad for slipping several into my purse.

My brain was static, as in immobile, as in a thin electric buzz. My desk was across from the conference room, which had a wall of picture windows. I trained my ears to hear commotion on the street, and I could tell traffic from protests from accidents. When the phone did ring, I jumped, startled. Everyone on the other end of the line heard my voice an octave higher than normal. Once in a while, Lily would come to my desk and hand me a packet to FedEx to the European office, and there was a momentary thrill in that, racing down to the courier's room in the service elevator with a thick envelope under my arm.

Once my restlessness wore off I was embarrassed. My thoughts were so boring! I tried to remember the name of a girl I sort of knew in college, and when I gave up, I texted somebody to ask. I decided not to cheat when trying to remember the name of her boyfriend, and as a result I've still forgotten him. Did I still remember all the state capitols? Yes. Could I list them in alphabetical order? Yes, after a day of practice. Sometimes my fingers would hover over the keyboard, and I'd eye a new word document, but the moment Lily heard me typing she'd step out of her office to check on me.

I sat in the silence, and then one day I bloomed, not like a flower, but like a teabag, steeping. There was silence seeping into me and I couldn't help but fill it back. Questions came into my consciousness and pictures followed to answer them, the saturation increasing slowly, developing before my mind's eye. Why didn't women carry eggs around in their mouths, like golden retrievers? Could I remember the prettiest shades of every color I ever saw? What if a man wanted to smell good so he drank perfume? Would I have been happier if I were a cowboy? I had not asked questions like this for a very long time.

At first I thought they came from nowhere. As time went on, I realized the questions were emerging from the silence. The silence, of course, was inside me, at this point. It somehow took months to know the questions came from me. The more nothing I did, the less logic the questions followed. In fact, I couldn't even tell what the questions were anymore. Images came one after another, erupting in vibrant detail, and I sat in a trance, working backwards to try and find out what I was answering.

Time passed quickly once I found my rhythm. My body was on autopilot, printing and binding presentations, but my mind was careening through new territory, unencumbered by sound or attention. The conference room where I assembled 1,890 holiday cards had a big-screen TV that I wasn't allowed to turn on, since it might impede my ability to hear the phone at the desk outside. My muscles cramped as I used a pair of scissors to make crisp folds in thick cardstock. Among the images in my mind, I began to see familiar faces. None of them were people I had met. While I peeled labels from adhesive sheets, I collected names, tucking some away for later, pairing others up with the people I was thinking of, wishing for the stickiness of recognition. When they fit perfectly, I felt a click behind my ear.

Silence wasn't something I would've chosen. But I surprised myself, becoming attached. No one in the office knew my name, but on days where my silence was uninterrupted, I went home feeling more firmly myself than ever before. The quiet got quieter: Janhavi went on business trips, Lily went on vacation. Caroline napped at her desk, sometimes leaving in the middle of the day to take lunch and returning after several hours. When it was just the two of us in the office, she lingered at my desk anytime she walked by, suddenly responsible. We were the same age and didn't attempt friendship, but sometimes she bound her own client presentations. I couldn't tell if she was sparing me the work or only trusted herself.

My silence grew, in and around me, and there was no-where for it to go. I sat with my hands spread over the freckled desk. During lunch breaks, and in the last thirty minutes of the day if everyone else left early, I would try to record what I had seen. Scribbling frantic notes with stolen pens, I crammed journals and paper-clipped scraps into my bag. Caroline asked why my purse was "always full of trash." At home, I had bigger notebooks, my own computer. On days when Janhavi was the only other person in the office, enclosed behind her locked door, I would spill everything into an email to myself, a line or two at a time throughout my shift, sending it to my personal address at the end of the day and deleting the missive from temp.admin.email's history.

In my real life, I began to want silence, too. I could no longer ignore urges that had always tugged at me. Mid-sentence, I would interrupt myself in conversation with a friend, sliding a notebook onto my lap and jotting down brief, broken lines. I missed train stops. I missed dinners. Every night in bed, I stared at the ceiling, willing myself awake, trying to assemble the answers and their questions into an order.

At Christmas, I mailed the last of the cards and went home to my family, paper cuts crisscrossing my creaky knuckles. By the time I got back, my hands were healed and the office was in disarray. Some interpersonal, political thing had happened, and everyone was off-kilter. Along with glaring and sighing, there was now stomping and slamming. Caroline left for long lunches and came back in house shoes. Janhavi took up whispering. Lily stood in front of her desk, tight-lipped, at the end of every day, staring out at midtown, gripping her backpack straps like there was a parachute inside. My silence was unsettled and so was I.

When they began to turn their little barbs into genuine

cruelties, I called my temp agency, not willing to be caught in crossfire. They arranged interviews before and after my workday. All my silence dried up, just like that. The office was hot with anger and I was sweaty with desperation. I couldn't wait to get out. My brain was fond of itself, and that quiet which made me so uneasy months ago. On the train home, my mind raced, sounds and sights strobing in warning, the onslaught of imagery flashing me into a panic.

I had an interview somewhere else – a normal interview, not a training – and the temp agency called me while I was on the way home. When they offered me the job, starting Monday, I told them about the terrible things I had overheard Caroline saying on the phone to London executives that morning, and asked not to return. They had been planning to cancel their contract with the investment firm, anyway. They would handle it.

I bought myself a few days at home, to "decompress," to mentally reset before I began my new job. I spent them sitting, cross-legged, comfortable, in my own home, with my own pens, my eyes blank as I held a séance on the page. My hand jerked across sheets of paper. I purged up the deep things. After I started the new job, I had downtime, and I spent it transposing now-familiar faces. Months went by and my life changed but the quiet was steady and clean. Silence, which lived inside me now, had given way to an abundance of language. When I think back on that job, what I liked about it best was nothing at all.

NOTICE ME
Emma Sloley

The pandemic put my vanity on pause. Confined for many months to the apartment I shared with my husband, I relinquished—like everyone else—all the little tokens of self-maintenance that involved other people. The haircuts, the manicures, the eyebrow shaping, the waxings. This isn't going to be one of those stories in which I discover and learn to cherish a more feral version of my usually put-together person. No rewilding of the self took place. I simply switched to performing those functions by myself, at home, with supermarket hair dye, boxed wax strips, magnifying mirrors and the like. The results weren't quite as good, because I'm no professional at these things, but it was fine. It was no sacrifice at all, really. No one in the household complained. Then why did I miss those little beauty maintenance outings so much? Why did the world feel so much smaller when I couldn't spend those minutes and hours in silence with some quick-fingered stranger smoothing all the rough edges of me into a pleasing new shape?

*

My vanity isn't new. I've cared deeply, even painfully, about the way I look since I was a kid. One of my most vivid childhood memories is of a dinner party thrown by my parents for their friends, in preparation for which I spent hours trying on different little outfits, agonizing over whether it was better to match my hair ribbon to my dress or whether that would seem to be trying too hard, as if a bunch of suburban booze-hounds were going to notice and appreciate the sartorial choices of an annoying, socially anxious ten-year-old. But it mattered to me, even back then, that I present my best self to the world. "I didn't notice you there," says a lawyer friend of my parents at the dinner party, laughing and ruffling my perfectly coiffured hair.

As I slouched into late teenagehood, the rituals became more elaborate and painstaking. (Less satisfying, too, compared to the innocent joy my ten-year-old self garnered from her preening, because I'd learned to thoroughly hate how I looked by then.) Not uncoincidentally, the best self I yearned toward in those years just happened to mirror the prevailing beauty standards of the time for women—highly feminine, lush-haired, rail-thin, carefully made up—and it was inevitable I'd carry this high-maintenance aesthetic into adulthood. My beauty rituals became tangled up with my sense of self, with the kind of person I wanted other people to see when they noticed me. But those same rituals came to have a secondary purpose.

It was only after we emerged from our hibernation that I began to understand what that purpose was, and what I'd been missing about those little beauty salon interactions. Not just the human touch, which so many people who endured the era in solitude lamented losing. It had to do with noticing. There was plenty to read about during those lost years, plenty of doom to scroll, but there weren't any venues available anymore in which to step outside my interior life. There wasn't anything to notice.

*

One time, a few years back, I was sitting in the swivel chair at the hair salon, waiting for the color to set. The stylist had gone off somewhere, leaving the timer ticking on the console next to me. My hair was ink-dark with dye and plastered to my skull. Bored of my magazine and detached for once from my phone, I watched in the mirror in ghoulish fascination as the minutes ticked down and I transformed ever-so-subtly from my recognizable self into a stranger. A weird-looking stranger with plastered-down purplish hair and rubbed-off makeup. That's when she appeared, a woman undergoing something subtle but seismic, awakening to her primal hidden self like an animal encountering the mirror test for the first time.

Those serendipitous moments were common in the before times. But I'd come close to forgetting they existed. Then last year, on a visit to New York—a place I once lived and bumped into all sorts of people both real and imagined—I decided to get my nails done. It was the first time in two years I'd entered a nail salon. As the technician bent over my neglected nail beds, I watched in a kind of rapture as a food show about cakes played silently on the huge flat screens lining the walls. I was there for more than an hour and the show just kept playing, a program with no discernible beginning or end, a permanent loop of white coated, hairnet-wearing humans moving through a factory space dedicated to the making and decorating of baroquely complicated cakes. Visions of frosting being extruded from stainless steel tubes and elaborate shapes being coaxed out of balls of dough danced across the screens like sweet hallucinations.

Because my mind was unoccupied with the usual concerns of my day—responding to emails, research, writing, doomscrolling—I found myself in a fully absorbent mental state, one in which I could minutely attend to whatever was happening in the world around me. It didn't matter that the thing in question was undeniably banal. It mattered that because I hadn't in any way sought it out or needed it, I was in a unique position to simply observe it. Alive to its possibilities.

*

The salons and clinics of my vanity rituals are a kind of third place for me, a site of coming together that is neither home nor office. Those little cathedrals of commerce are sacred spaces in which I open myself to new possibilities, the "what ifs?" of the imagination that roll past like cakes on a conveyor belt. Getting out of my house, out of own head, away from the attention-hogging screens of my daily routine and into these third places feels crucial to the project of taking notice.

Of course I could go for a walk in the park instead, take a hike, look at trees, submerge myself in the ocean, and I love to do all those things. I know lots of creative people for whom those incursions into nature are nourishing, even essential, in putting them into the perfect mental space for creativity to take root. But for me, those natural places are nourishing but too meditative, even soporific. When I'm in nature I want to zoom out, not in.

It's in the places dedicated to beautifying where I can hone in. When I sit in front of the hairdresser's mirror, or joggle around in the aggressively vigorous nail salon massage chair, it's as if I'm finally ready to receive all those messages. I'm ready to notice.

ALLEYMAN
Kevin Maloney

I. Emphysema, or The Road not Taken

Shortly after my 30th birthday, I went to the doctor for the first time in over a decade. He asked me a lot of questions and frowned at my answers. *Cigarettes?* Yes. *How many?* Oh geez. Pack a day, maybe? Sometimes more depending on how much I've been drinking. *Alcohol?* Ha, definitely. I'm not sure how much. I usually lose track after my fourth or fifth shot of Old Crow.

My doctor made me breathe into a tube that spit out something that looked like receipt tape. He frowned again and said I had emphysema. Sort of. If I quit smoking, what I had would probably go away. But if I continued, then what I had would be called emphysema.

I was recently divorced and dating for the first time since my early 20s. I imagined my profile pic with plastic tubes snaked up my nose. Resting my oxygen tank on the stool next to me as I tried to make small talk at the bar. Smoking was supposed to make me look like James Dean in *Rebel Without a Cause,* not Dennis Hopper in *Blue Velvet.*

I decided to get healthy. I threw my American Spirits away and slapped a 21 mg nicotine patch on my arm. I started doing sit-ups and lifting concrete cinderblocks in my backyard. I made rules for myself to cut down on my drinking:

1) no hard stuff, only beer

2) no drinking before 5 p.m.

3) never buy more than two beers at a time

My plan worked. I stopped coughing from the moment I woke up until I went to sleep at night. I noticed I could smell things again. I spent less time puking up cheap whiskey and half-digested bean burritos and more time sitting on my couch, sipping coffee, wondering what to do with my life.

The only problem was that I was never happy with just two beers a night. I really needed that third beer, but that meant another trip to the store. I drank green tea and stared at the wall and tried to think about something other than beer, which only made me think more about beer. Eventually I caved and left on another beer run.

At the time, I lived about ten blocks from New Seasons, Portland's overpriced hippie grocery store. I had a car, but according to my doctor there was a thing called exercise that I needed to do occasionally to avoid cancer, heart attacks, and a number of other terrifying diseases. Eventually, I made a fourth rule:

4) beer runs by foot only

I grabbed my wallet and my keys and walked out my back door, which abutted an alleyway—one in a series connecting my apartment building to New Seasons.

When most people picture an alley, they think of New York City: brick, dumpsters, rats, garbage, steam coming out of manholes. Portland's alleys are the verdant, weed-strewn opposite. Imagine a hobbit Shire if every hobbit kept backyard chickens. Smurf Village if Smurfette had tattoo sleeves and was captain of her roller derby team. The alleys stretch about ten feet across, offering a mostly impassible lane of muddy ruts with puddles inside. Fences sag under the weight of Himalayan blackberries. Ferns grow from abandoned gas cans.

A dozen or more times a week I traversed this path on my way to beer, leaving my apartment empty-handed, returning with my pair of tall boys, feeling like a glorious, troubled hunter. All my pleasure-centers fired at once: first in anticipation of beer, then in my selection of beer, then walking home with my IPAs beaded in sweat, listening to Neil Young on my earbuds.

II. Urban Voyeurism

At first, my beer runs were purely functional, but over time, alley walking bled into other areas of my life. Whenever I had to go anywhere within walking distance, I left on foot and scoped out the hidden dirt paths between houses, trying to find the strangest, least trodden route.

Each alley offered something different. Some had well maintained back fences, giving the alley a feeling of being cut off from the world. These alleys were like nature preserves. Fording their thickets, I came upon bird and yellow jacket nests, garter snakes and butterflies. Other alleys were lined by chain link fences or no fences at all, offering a voyeuristic view into people's backyards.

This was 2008, three years before *Portlandia* convinced a million tattooed yuppies from New York and LA to swoop in with their hot yoga and toddlers, turning Alberta Street into a nursery for the skinny jean elite. In 2008, the neighborhood was still a mix of artists, urban farmers, and the longtime residents of this historically black neighborhood being displaced by the influx of artists and urban farmers. It was a problem rooted in Portland's racist past, but for a few years, before developers tore down all the beautiful old Craftsmen, replacing them with homogenous skinny houses, it made for incredible yard gazing.

On my walks, I saw baby goat pens, rusted patio furniture, outdoor bathtubs, galleries of metal yard art, trampolines, a competitive rose garden, Jesus statues, DIY puppet show theaters, children's play structures, and dog kennels with multiple angry pit bulls inside. Some backyards were the work of hoarders with junk organized into careful piles: televisions, kitchenware, electronics, children's dolls. One yard showed the evidence of a former order and pride gone feral. I imagined elderly inhabitants. A husband who'd lost his wife to cancer. Divorce. The death of a child.

The most interesting yards, to me, were out of sync with themselves. A perfectly ordered front yard with chaos in back. Indicating... what? That its occupants were just barely holding it together for appearances? Other houses were the exact opposite: neglect in front, a little Eden in back. "Fuck all of you!" I imagined its owner saying. "I'm going to hide back here while the world burns to the ground."

III. Here Be Dragons

My first alley wasn't a real alley. It was more of a drainage ditch between backyards—a no man's land of corrugated pipe, dandelions, and scotch broom, surrounded by fence on three and a half sides... a mistake of suburban planning visible from the sidewalk where I walked back and forth to grade school every day. It was littered with empty beer bottles and condom wrappers, suggesting a darkness lurking behind the façade of our cookie cutter suburban neighborhood.

As kids, we heard legends about transgressions committed in the alley: drugs, sex acts, fistfights, witchcraft. It was in reference to this alley and a certain friend's older sister that I first heard the expression, "He popped her cherry." I went home that night and trembled under the covers. What was a cherry? Did I have one, and if so, would somebody pop it one day? What happened next—would I die?

At night, I dreamed of the alley. I pictured disfigured spirits lurking in the weeds. Dead bodies stashed in those corrugated pipes. Escaped convicts camping among the yellow flowers. As a teenager, I thought of the alley when I read the opening scene of Stephen King's *It*—Georgie Denbrough following his paper boat to a storm drain where he's accosted by Pennywise, the timeless demonic clown.

The alley was the closest thing our neighborhood had to *terra incognita*—the cartography term for an uncharted region. Or as the medieval mapmakers wrote, HC SVNT DRACONES, "Here be dragons," referring to the tradition of drawing sea monsters at the edges of maps.

In a region as meticulously laid out as a 1980s suburb, we only had this one aberration: a city engineer's oversight. A dead zone that allowed us, in a small way, to believe in monsters.

IV. A Vision of Death

The first time my son Fennel flew across the country to spend the summer with me at my apartment in Northeast Portland, I was excited to share my newfound love of alleys. Our first Saturday together, I filled my thermos with beer, and gave Fennel his own kid-sized thermos filled with hot chocolate. We walked out the back door of our apartment, ducked through the gate, and hung a hard right into that beautiful mess of half-collapsed fences, blackberry brambles, and feral cats.

KEVIN MALONEY

Like most 6-year-olds, Fennel was disinterested in exercise. I'd lured him with the promise of kittens. The often-pregnant alley cat had recently given birth to a litter of four furry babies. I'd brought a metal mixing bowl along and picked blackberries as we went, but Fennel ran ahead. At the end of the alley, he came upon the pile of wooden pallets, behind which lay the mama cat. Two of the kittens furiously sucked her nipples. One black kitten approached us, unafraid even though it was only a few weeks old. A fourth kitten lay off to the side, seemingly sleeping.

Fennel got down on all fours and held out his hand. The black kitten mewed and sniffed his fingers. I stood back with my harvest of berries, ready to receive my Father of the Year award.

"What's wrong with that one?" asked Fennel, pointing at the small gray kitten sleeping off to the side.

"What do you mean?" I asked.

"Why's it covered in flies?"

I set my blackberries down and looked closer. The kitten was alive, but barely. Its eyes were oozing some creamy yellow substance. It was smaller than its siblings. When I approached it, it barely acknowledged me. It held on with a fluttering heart and small breaths.

"It's the runt," I said.

"What's that?" asked Fennel.

"The mom only has so much milk. She gives it to the stronger kittens. This kitten isn't getting enough. It's going to die."

As I said it, it occurred to me that it was true. This kitten would be dead by tomorrow, putting a serious damper on what I hoped would be a summer of father-son alley bonding. The flies were 24 hours early, feasting on the kitten's eye infection. When the poor thing took its last breath, they'd move on to the more delicious morsels.

A better father would have used this as a civics lesson and called animal control to put the kitten to sleep. But I hated authority figures, and animal control was a little too close to a cop for my liking. I imagined being interrogated: "Why were you in the alley? Why did you bring your son into this filthy place?"

"Because I was raised in the suburbs," I'd say. "There are dragons here."

"Let's take it home," said Fennel.

"It's too late," I said. "He's full of diseases."

Fennel started crying. I was a bad father. I took my son by the hand and dragged him back to our apartment. He kicked and screamed the whole way, begging for the life of the dead kitten. We ate cereal covered in blackberries. Fennel sipped hot chocolate from his thermos, glaring at me.

The following Saturday, despite a lot of protest, I convinced Fennel to have another go at the alley. This time, there were only three kittens. Fennel named them Silver, Midnight, and Dead Cat's Sister. On the way home, we became momentarily enshrouded in a cloud of ladybugs.

V. Things I Have Seen on My Alley Walks

1) A man sleeping in his lawn chair, surrounded by empty beer bottles, dangerously sunburned.

2) A real bird perched on a stone bird perched on a stone St. Francis statue.

3) An elderly woman in a bathrobe, leaning over, petting her cat, saying, "I love you so much! You're such a good cat. Do you even know how beautiful you are?"

4) A family of raccoons peering down at me from a tree, wearing robber masks, plotting crimes.

5) The chain that usually held my neighbor's Rottweiler at bay, broken, no dog in sight.

VI. Alleys Are Drugs For People
Who Don't Do Drugs (Anymore)

There's a theory among certain drug gurus that the human brain is primarily an editing machine, limiting information to only what is necessary for survival. Using psychedelics, they reason, is like firing the editor for 4 - 6 hours. Suddenly we fathom all information coming to us through our senses: the known and unknown, important and insignificant, ripped of meaning and purpose. Holy, as it really is.

In my 20s, I loved eating psilocybin mushrooms, wrapping my arms around rhododendron bushes and weeping at their beauty. But at some point, I had too many friends who'd blasted their brains on the stuff and turned into slobbering misfits. I tried to find other ways to crack open my third eye.

Walking in alleys is the closest thing I've found. So much of our lives are preoccupied by getting to and from somewhere. Usually work. We drive on highways with their black asphalt and yellow lines, everyone honking, nobody ever getting there fast enough. In the few precious hours remaining to us, we drink to numb the pain of pissing our lives away, honking at each other, never getting anywhere fast enough. Leaving the road, ducking behind the shrubs, squeezing through the chain-link fence and finding yourself in a useless world is like becoming flooded by reality at the expense of survival. It's the world from the vantage point of God.

To walk in alleys is to fire the editor for a few hours, a chance to peel back the veneer and take in everything.

VII. Just a While Longer

A few years ago, I moved to the St. Johns neighborhood of Portland. There aren't as many alleys here as there are in other parts of the city. Or there are, but they're wider, almost roads themselves: unpaved paths 50 feet across, covered with gravel, pocked by 18-inch potholes. The thing about St. Johns, though, the streets themselves are narrow. Other than a few busy thoroughfares, every road feels like an alley.

I like it this way. After fifteen years obsessed with alley walking, the world has become an alley. Front and back yards are indistinguishable. I walk down the sidewalk and see people doing openly what I used to see them doing only in secret. Nothing unsavory. Just tender moments: talking to cats and birds, walking around in bathrobes, surveying overgrown lawns, too old to push a mower around, too poor to hire someone to do it for them.

The other day, my wife and I were on one of these walks together. She stops at every house with a cat in the yard. Our walks sometimes last hours. She stopped at one house with four cats in the driveway. She called to them. They ran to her and head-butted her legs, then flopped on the ground, exposing their bellies. She scratched them and told them how beautiful they were.

My wife had a cancer scare this year. That is, she had cancer... a small nodule in her thyroid. For a while, the doctors thought it had spread to her lymph nodes, but it turned out it hadn't. They cut out half her thyroid and sewed her back together. Hopefully that's the end of it. But it was scary—all that uncertainty.

It rained every day this April. The shrubs were overwhelmed. They didn't know what to do with all that water, so they channeled it into their flowers. The limbs sagged under the weight, covered in pink ballerinas.

We don't get enough time on this planet. Just when we figure out how to slow the whole thing down for a few seconds and get a good look at it, our bodies pull a gun on us from the inside.

Not yet, we beg them. *Just a little while longer.*

For today, our prayers are working. We walk among cats and old ladies, taking everything in, whispering as we walk: *thank you thank you thank you.*

On Perserverance

BUCKETS
Mitchell Nobis

I grew up on a dairy farm. We had a basketball hoop on the side of the old milking parlor, the one we used for storage after my grandpa, dad, and uncle had the new one built in '76. I haven't worked on the farm in twenty years, but back then, we still called the '76 parlor "the new one." Farmers don't love change.

My big brother and I shot hoops, or whatever must have approximated shooting hoops without training. My dad played football at Western. (Walked on as an offensive lineman and ended up playing a lot. Pretty badass, really.) My mom was athletic then too, but neither of them played basketball. Still, they must have showed us or we figured out the general idea of heaving a basketball skyward. I was too young to get it to the hoop most of the time, but I kept trying. We shoveled away snow in winter, chucked the ball ten feet high and watched it thud on the concrete, too cold to bounce.

At some point, there was a basketball camp put on by the varsity coach and his squad. The gym gleamed compared to the side of the old milking parlor. The backboards shined under bright lights, and the rims glowed orange like fire. I learned a proper jump shot. I learned to box out. I learned to crossover, to spin, to bring up the same-side hand and knee on layups. I learned how to see both your player and the ball on defense. I worked on the fundamentals. The head coach called me "Dr.

N," and this being the pre-Jordan '80s, a Dr. J reference was the hippest damn thing you could get. I was hooked.

My dad put a basketball hoop in our backyard. A better one, on a pole, not on the side of a milking parlor. They poured a cement pad. The deep corners were just far enough to be three-pointers. I lived in those corners.

I shot buckets. I shot a lot of buckets. My brother started to work on the farm, so I spent my middle school and early high school years shooting more buckets, both by myself but also with him when he wasn't working. Our family played two-on-two often. When friends came over, we held tournaments, and when we had an odd number of guys, we played 21 or Commando. Basketball became a form of breathing.

I made the freshmen and JV teams, but since I was slow and clumsy and had more success as a drummer, I didn't try out for varsity. I spent more time on drums. It turns out I should have tried out and done both, but you can't be wise before the mistake. I kept playing on my own and in intramurals. I started working on the farm too, but I'd still find time to shoot buckets, a boombox blasting Public Enemy or Kool Moe Dee. I'd play pickup games when I could, but I lived five miles out of town. Somehow, my brother and I found out about an underground weekly pickup game in Maple Rapids, where some local kids broke into the church gym every Sunday night. I was a late bloomer, and it was there, my senior year of high school, where my body started to click and shots in motion started to fall. Still, that was only one hour per week. I mostly hooped in solitude.

In college, I kept playing whenever I could, but I'd also learned the meditation of shooting by then. I'd find empty park courts, more comfortable most days getting shots up than playing in a game. Competition became a corollary—

fun, sure, but not the point. One day, I was shooting three pointers on a short park court, so they looked like half-court shots. An old man from the neighborhood stopped with his dog and said, "Glen Rice used to do that here all the time." This was five years after Michigan won the men's basketball tournament, where Rice was the star. He was successful in the NBA already then, and most of the Fab Five had just moved on too. I shot a few dozen extra shots that day. Fundamentals: square up, bend the knees, spring upward, snap the wrist on the follow through.

Our intramural teams got spanked. We played pickup ball at the IM too, where my buddies considered me our best player, and a team where I'm the best player gets beaten in one minute flat by a team with a U-M guy running with them. But any day with basketball is a good day, I told myself, and I kept playing.

I became a teacher. I'd play with the other staff at 6am once or twice a week. I had a career cumulative one hour of actual game minutes on my own school teams, but somehow I became a coach for a short time, mostly as an assistant. I would bark about fundamentals over and over, convinced they were the road to success. I lost my voice shouting "RE-BOUND" at every shot. My coaching career was spent yelling "REBOUND." I knew rebounding got you another chance. Rebounding always got you another chance.

Some 25 years into a teaching career, I still play basketball. My wife and I put a hoop and a pad of cement in our back-yard when our boys were eight- and four-years-old. We have photos of them hiding in the hole I dug for the basketball hoop post, poking their heads up to see the bright world. Now I teach my boys to shoot. I show them how to keep their legs under them, to keep the elbow in. I show them, over and over, the fundamentals. I still practice them myself when I can, but I realize now that I've spent most of my time showing others how to play. I get in some ball where I can—I play on rec league teams that mostly lose, but, still, every free throw is nirvana. Every swish is a prayer.

I keep shooting, less than I wish I could. I still play whenever I can. When my jumper goes wonky, I break it back down to the studs. I put it back together. I start over. I rebuild, knowing what I should do and countering my shoddy body every time it strays. I do my best in dwindling minutes. I don't know how to measure success when I was never going to be good enough to play professional ball in the first place. I don't know what success even means. I never knew to worry about it until an end was in sight, but now it is and now I worry but worry is all I know to do. I keep shooting in the meantime. It's the only prayer I have.

SEE TOM RUN
Abigail Oswald

I have now seen every Tom Cruise movie thanks to Covid-19. I am a person who gives myself projects—or, as I see it, mild distractions from pervasive existential dread—and a global pandemic that forced us all inside our homes as the world shuddered to a unified halt called for one mighty distraction indeed. Mine, as it turned out, just so happened to take the form of a movie star.

In those early months I watched Tom run across landscapes decimated by explosions and aliens, football fields and sand dunes, hospital halls and city streets. He ran beside trains and down escalators and across the sides of buildings. Sometimes he was running away from something; sometimes he was the one giving pursuit. He ran through the future and the past. As I watched through Tom's filmography, I began to feel as if he was running for all of us, enclosed as we were within our walls.

*

The first time the world met Tom Cruise, he was running. He made his film debut in the 1981 adaptation of *Endless Love* as Billy, a young soccer-playing arsonist whose entire appearance doesn't even clock a full minute. He runs into the shot, an early '80s prototype in cutoff denim shorts and a blue tank-top. Even then, he stands out from the rest; the camera follows him as he separates from the team to join his friends. Watching now, it almost seems as if the very force of his presence magnetizes the camera, pulling our collective gaze in a new direction. A bit part, you might think, yet one that alters the course of the story—the film's pivotal house fire stems from just a few lines of his dialogue. Tom was redirecting narratives even from the beginning.

*

On YouTube there's an almost nineteen-minute compilation of Tom running. The edit pulls from no less than twenty-three of Tom's films, spanning 1981 to 2015: thirty-four years of sprinting collected in a single video clip. Genre is irrelevant; you might be inclined to think first of Tom's action films—*Mission Impossible, Minority Report*—but Tom runs just as fast in *Far and Away, All the Right Moves*. The running happens in every kind of movie; it is the thing that connects his disparate stories together. A common thread through everything, his uniting theme. With each close-up, I wonder: What keeps him going? And I don't mean his characters—not Ethan or Jack, Vincent or Lestat—but *Tom*.

*

There's a film called *Millennium Actress* in which the protagonist runs throughout all the roles of her career toward the same thing—the same person, in fact. An artist who gave her a crucial gift in her youth and then abruptly vanished, never to be seen again. No matter what character the actress plays, whatever time period she's reenacting, she seeks the same goal in the end. Sometimes her ardor is so palpable that it feels as if she's trying to outrun time itself. At a certain point so many years have passed that it feels more like she is searching for an idea than a person.

Since first seeing this movie I have thought about Tom Cruise in the same way. In theory, there must be some endpoint. A moment when he could finally rest. But does that point exist in the future, or the past? Is the goal he's chasing even possible, is it real?

*

There are two parts of running, of course: what lies behind you, and what you are moving toward. Running becomes a means of focusing, always something coming closer and something else receding into the distance. Escape and pursuit at once, moving toward some real or imagined point on the horizon.

Even as Tom runs, he is trying to run faster still, endlessly chasing excellence. Maybe he is not unlike the protagonist of *Millennium Actress*, in the end. Running after an impossible ideal, which by default he can only pursue, never reach.

*

Tom spent several weeks on a treadmill for the filming of *Eyes Wide Shut*; New York appears on a screen behind him via a technique called rear projection. It sounds like an urban legend until you Google it and see the pictures: Tom on the treadmill in his trench coat and lace-up shoes. The story goes that Kubrick refused to travel, so they created a dreamlike illusion of Manhattan on the other side of the ocean via lights, soundstage, and exercise equipment.

Was Tom going anywhere? No. But he kept moving.

*

There is a way that all actors tell you who they are through the characters they play. In showcasing their range via a vast spectrum of personalities, some might show you all the people they are not. But there are others who give us pieces of themselves through the ways in which the roles they choose begin to overlap. A single actor can create a narrative across all their collected films, the kinds of stories they return to. Perhaps we will never know this actor, really, but we might come to recognize the person they pretend to be. I like to imagine they are all learning a little more about themselves this way, too. The choices we make in art—in life—reveal us to ourselves and others.

There's a thread of earnestness throughout almost all of Tom's roles that says something about him. You get the sense, every time, that he is in a world of his own. That he is perhaps picturing a finished project which is somehow different, better, and beyond what everyone else around him is attempting to create. And he is always pushing himself a little bit harder. Trying to make this perfect thing, which by the nature of its creation will always somehow still be flawed.

*

I once read an interview in which the subject commented that a film is never so good as before its premiere. Prior to that day it exists in the audience's minds as a web of conjecture, hype, and viral stills. All its shiniest parts are spliced together in the trailer; the plot holes do not yet exist; the public's reaction is still entirely hypothetical. But once the film is released in its entirety, there's nothing left to reveal. Now the audience can pick the story apart, the critics can write their reviews. Original intent matters less and less. Yet there's something enduringly romantic about the way a film exists as an idea, before all of that—for this is what keeps us going. The dream that we might make exactly what we envisioned and have the chance to share it with the world.

Perhaps none of it will ever quite be what Tom wanted—the stunt, the scene, the film. And once it is out in the world, people are free to make of it whatever they will—to remove it from its context, to apply all manner of critical lenses. To hate it. To love it. It's a complete surrender of control, and that final step has little to do with Tom Cruise at all.

What a powerful, terrifying idea—to create something, and then to let it go.

*

Does Tom accept, when he runs, that the scene will never be perfect? Maybe he believes in the possibility of perfection, and maybe that is what he has pursued for decades now with such persistent fervor.

Perhaps you can strive toward that goal, always challenging yourself, but that's not the point, is it? The point is to find a way to live with the imperfection, to find a kind of beauty in it. And maybe the answer then—for Tom, for all of us—is to keep going. To know every time you will fail, and to try anyway.

And so Tom runs.

LAUNDRY
Amie Souza Reilly

This morning, as on so many mornings, I sorted the largest pile into smaller, more manageable piles. Towels. Sheets. Dark colors. Lights. I dragged those more manageable piles into our basement, which is dark, a little damp, full of stuff we need and stuff we don't. And though I hate the house centipedes that sleep in the corners, I do not mind the long-bodied spiders that hum as they wrap their prey in webbing. Mostly I remember to check pants pockets before I throw them in. Once, when I didn't remember, the ten-pass train ticket I needed to get me back and forth to grad school stayed in my pocket, came out soaked and blurred and useless, one hundred and thirty-four dollars turned to pulp. I have washed Lego pieces, toy cars, tissues. I have washed as many things that shouldn't be washed as I have things that must be.

Our washing machine has a weight sensor, which works to, somehow, determine the right amount of water needed to wash our clothes without any excess. It was expensive, more than we would have normally paid, but our old one stopped working and this was the only model in stock. We couldn't go weeks waiting for a less expensive machine, so we bought it. I don't regret it, though I do sometimes feel guilty.

The dryer, however, is old. It seems to dry clothes purely out of habit. It makes too much noise, thuds and clunks that I know mean there is a larger problem, that, for now, can be ignored. On occasion I have hung things to dry, outside, on the line, but too quickly became embarrassed by what strangers could see, might surmise, about me. Unless we get another dryer, I will be vigilantly gentle turning the rusted knob. I will remember to clean the lint trap.

Some say that they lose socks in the dryer. I know it is not possible to lose them—matter cannot be created or destroyed—but they do seem to disappear. When our dog died, I washed her blankets over and over, not trying to wash her out, but because I knew if I kept washing them I didn't have to throw them away. I still haven't thrown them away, they sit in the trunk of my car, with me through much of my day.

Her hair, too, stays in these machines, clings to our laundry. She turns up in the cuff of a sweater or threaded through the eyehook on a bra. Even if I wanted not to think of her, she is there.

What is first washed, then dried, must be folded. Warm, I run my hands over flannel button-downs, over well-loved t-shirts, smoothing wrinkles, folding neat stacks. Towels into thirds. Sheets, though difficult, wrangled into squares. Each sock with its mate, rolled into a ball.

Even when I am done with the laundry I am not. I am wearing clothes, my husband, our child, all with clothes on. Underwear, sweatpants, shorts, jeans, pajamas, the knit hat our teen wears in an effort to smooth out a head full of unruly curls, my husband's handkerchief, nearly sheer. I have dropped an English muffin, butter side down, on the thigh of my favorite green pants, and so, the laundry must start again.

There is satisfaction, of course, in taking the dank, the foul-smelling, and making it fresh. Though I find it hard to find any joy in the putting away of the clean laundry. It is clean, to the best of my ability, the butter stain will never fully come out, and so I must put it in drawers, in closets, in piles on the chair. Once put away, my work seems inconsequential.

But it is not.

To do the laundry is to be the keeper of intimate secrets. Underwear stretched, mysterious stains. To do the laundry is to be privy to the mess of being alive. Only those who love you most are willing to see, to touch, those secrets and still want to be near you after.

I am almost forty-three and I feel as if I have been trying to finish the laundry for most of my adult life. To get to a point where it is all washed, dried, folded, put away. It has not yet happened. Perhaps it never will. Perhaps that is the best part—these details of our lives, so mundane, so repetitive, like sunrises and tides and heartbeats, are proof we are alive.

NOT TO MENTION THE PARKING
Katie Darby Mullins

When everything has already gone to hell, you can count on the parking at the University of Evansville to make it worse. Professors have limited options, but the best one— that is, if you are someone who can some days run up to five miles and some days, still need a cane from that stroke you had a few years back, right after you turned 31– is "the oval." This is about forty highly competitive spots on a circular parallel parking hellscape. Lucky for me, I did have a stroke, so I get to compete for one of the awesome and more available handicapped parking spots, which is useful because teaching takes all I have (and sometimes, as Tom Petty would say, a little more).

I am also always running late. I used to have business cards that didn't say my profession or any titles, just my name and "Sorry I'm Late!" under it. Usually that was enough to defuse a situation. I should get more of those business cards, but I'm afraid the joke would grow stale. Everyone in my life knows I'm late. My mother once told me she thought it was a kind of (what I think of as "perverse") optimism— that I always thought I could get everywhere and do everything and one more task would fit. That is a very nice way of saying this is not a new problem.

So I'm running late to an intro survey lit/writing class and it's been a rough semester. This is my second semester with masks, my fourth with Covid running rampant. I lost the vision in my left eye from teaching on Zoom, so I don't have great vision to start with, and since the stroke, face blindness has rendered me unable to recognize my own face in the mirror, so good luck everybody else. But this has been a particularly low tempo year. I don't know why I can't get the right energy going. I'm trying. They're trying. But there's a disconnect. I couldn't pay them to talk— partially because I don't have the money, and partially because none of them would find that to be a good trade. And I am trying not to think about how I'm about to go up the hill backwards again when I get stuck in a funeral procession.

This happens a few times a week. I pass, not kidding, three funeral homes on the way to work. I always try to say to myself, "They are having a worse day than you," and while that's true, the blurry clock in the car reminds me I am already late. But that's not really the problem today. I am worried my husband is sick again. Last time he was sick, it took years and five surgeries, and none of it was easy for him. The hearse pulls out in front of me and I burst into tears.

Finally, I get to work and go to turn into the oval—there are blockades in front of the oval.

I'm not kidding. It's a Friday in April and I am going to have to learn a new place to park.

You have to have balls to walk into your own classroom ten minutes late, clearly having just cried, and to say, "OK, shut up," to a completely silent room. This is what I tell myself as I do it every single day. I've got a Dallas Cowboys cup in my right hand (because I like to think that even when I'm losing, I can pretend I'm a winner and that's just as good), even though I never move my mask in class. Clearly, my body is already a lemon. Clearly, my husband is immunocompromised. The mask stays up, and the Cowboys cup taunts me all class, full of water I won't drink.

"OK, shut up," I say. No laughs. It hasn't gotten a laugh all year. I pretend I'm Andy Kaufman and that I actually don't want them to laugh. "I've been thinking a lot. We've been reading vulnerable stories and poems and discussing our thoughts on them, but we haven't really been vulnerable ourselves. And we are all pushed so far beyond what we feel capable of, I can't imagine any of us can sleep at night." Then I hear the catch in my voice. "I didn't sleep last night."

A few people nod and all the sudden, I'm not climbing up the hill anymore, I am Sisyphus and the rock has rolled down over me, and I can't shut up. "My husband might be sick. I'm terrified." I never talk about him being sick. "I'm stressed. I'm overwhelmed. I know that everyone expects me to do more than I ever have for less, and that I'm supposed to be grateful for it. I know that society actively dismisses you and your generation, but you were literally raised in a bubble for a few years, and that can't be good for you. And then I got here today, and the fucking parking—"

And then I know how to get them to talk. "OK, you know what? For ten minutes, before your workshop group talks, I want every single person to say something that's stressing it out. And after you've said it and the words evaporate, the problem will disappear," I say.

A laugh. I got a laugh.

Holy fuck.

"The problem can be big," I said. "My husband starting to feel some familiar symptoms. That's big. But it could be small. Because it was the parking that broke me."

A kid who has literally never spoken before says, "The parking here sucks."

Everyone laughs. I loudly agree, with ebullient profanity, and then I decide to close the door. "Ten minutes. But it's an all-play. Remember, the stakes can be as low as the parking."

That's the trick about stakes, isn't it? They're an emotional stock market. Something that's not high stakes one day, like the feral cats that scream outside my bedroom at night, might be the thing that makes me absolutely lose my mind the next. It depends on whether or not I've had sleep or I'm able to use my physical body to run and move or if I ate Taco Bell, which always makes things worse except for the fifteen delicious minutes of eating. Some days, I am annoyed by the ants that are in the kitchen. Sometimes, I call it a Holy War. I'm not kidding.

I'm changing everyone's names here, because what happened next was magical and depended completely on how the first few students' went. I figured everyone would say a sentence or two, but the first speakers were sincere and had very real problems. Disability services wasn't working with one student who was told it would be easier if she was all the way blind. One student was dealing with finals for one of the most notoriously difficult arts classes in the university, but apologized for saying that, because it wasn't a "real problem." We all loudly assured them, yes, it is a real problem, and none of us were jealous of their finals.

"I think we'll find that as bad as our problems are, few of us would trade for the unknown," I finally say. "Your problems might suck, but they're yours, and you own them. That gives you a little control." I am surprised at how many people immediately agree.

Then the magic happens. Enter E.

"OK, so," they say, hopping into the windowsill to sit down and tell the whole story. I want to hug them more than I have ever wanted to hug someone. "My parents are getting divorced."

Everyone immediately goes to comfort them, but they

wave it off. It is kind of brilliant. "That's not my thing!" they protest. "I've got a real thing!"

So we're laughing at divorce now. And I can tell this is going to take more than ten minutes, but I have to see where this goes.

"I have to graduate in a few weeks, and my dad calls and asks what times he can see me, and what times my mom can." Keep in mind, reader, every single person in the room is starting to get involved. We are actively *Mystery Science Theatre*-ing this story. Cheering when E. gets a good punchline, loudly protesting when we feel they've been wronged. You'll just have to read our Greek chorus in, yourself. Maybe you should actively moan and laugh, too.

"I'm like, OK, great, this isn't stressful enough. But I try and figure it out. I start asking around, I get plans made with my partner, I figure out how to work moving out in with having them not see each other, and I call him back and tell him he gets breakfast. Then I tell my mom she gets lunch, and she says, 'Why can't we all do something together?'"

OK, here we all say, "aww." In a master stroke of storytelling, though, E. has tricked us. "So I have to say, 'Uhh. I'm sorry, Dad doesn't want to.' And I feel like shit! Until she says, 'Oh. Can I bring Chad?'"

We rioted.

Another girl points and yells, "My parents are getting divorced, but my mom's is named Danny!"

We decide Chad and Danny should meet at graduation. They should form a small, weird club. They're going to need someone to talk to. They're going to have some stressful days coming.

E. had some other (major) stressors, and we talked about all of them. I couldn't help myself. We were all so taken by the reveal that the dad wasn't being a dick that we wanted to hear everything. I can't tell you how many people in that room were dealing with loved ones who had cancer, pets who were nearing the end of their lives, breakups and breakdowns. But they were all ultra-vulnerable about it. I kept saying, "Remember guys. Parking is an acceptable complaint." Before long, everyone's story ends with, "Well. And the parking. Not to mention the parking."

One student says, "I'm actually doing better this year than last year," like she's apologizing, and we all tell her it takes real strength to own that she's doing something right. She beams. Then she says, "I'm a little scared because I have three finals on one day next week, though."

"You can get that rescheduled," the young man who had, again, literally never spoken, says. "I can tell you how."

All of the sudden, people start helping each other with their problems. There are tiny side conversations after each airing of the grievances. I regret that I don't have a Festivus Pole, and then I regret thinking that because they are young enough that they would not have any idea what the reference was. I think about the funeral procession again. There's so much to do between this and that.

Most people stayed at least a half hour late. Six or seven stayed over an hour late. Two or three stayed for two hours. I learned more about my students that day than I had in an entire semester, and the best part was that I like them. I liked every single one of them. They had wicked senses of humor, good storytelling abilities, generous hearts that were full of pain for people— because they loved those people. There were no small stakes. There were no complaints that weren't vulnerable. Even the parking, it winds up, because that says, "I am at my breaking point and I don't know what to do anymore. I don't have a place, not even here."

When some people had to leave for another class at the end of our class period, I apologized. I said, "I'm so sorry to have wasted an hour I know you work hard to pay for. I'm sorry I didn't teach you anything." I got so many emails and very genuine comments assuring me that it had been a very useful class period. That's what I'm always striving for anyway, right? To be useful to them?

I hit another funeral procession on my way home, and it was a lot easier to laugh off: I know I'll have a parking spot, and hopefully by the time I get home, Andy will have heard from his rheumatologist. For the rest of the slow ride behind a hearse and a row of mourners, just knowing that no matter what, my problems are mine, and I get to decide how high or low the stakes are, will have to be enough.

On Living a Writing Life

KNIT, PURL
Ellen Rhudy

The first scarf I knitted—wow, is it bad. Too itchy to wear, also a little too short to wear. Lay it flat on a table and you can see how its edges are all wonky, wobbling in and out as I tried to get the tension right. "Hold the yarn tighter," I kept thinking as I worked on the scarf, scared the yarn would simply fall off the needle if I didn't maintain this constant tension. It would be another year before I understood the yarn didn't have to be so tight it squeaked as I pushed it along the needle, that "tension" didn't require holding the yarn tight but simply, you know, holding it.

*

For years my mother wanted me to knit. Through the nineties she was always in her rocking chair, a tote bag of yarn under the side table, clicking away on a sweater. Repeatedly during my childhood, she taught me one stitch (knit), and I would make an eighth or a quarter of a teddy bear-sized scarf before getting bored and giving up. I didn't want to knit. I wasn't *interested* in knitting. Then I was twenty-six or twenty-seven and I was interested. I disliked my job and was straining for some type of creative outlet. For my birthday, she paid for knitting lessons.

*

There are two styles of knitting: English and continental. There was no discussion of this at my knitting class; we were simply taught the English style because it's most common in America. Having a Danish mother, though, I'd grown up inculcated in continental knitting. Despite my childhood resistance, my sense that I had no more idea of how to knit than someone who'd never held a pair of needles, in class I proved myself incapable of throwing the yarn over my needle in the American (the English) style. I couldn't get comfortable holding my needles and yarn. Between lessons, I FaceTimed my mother, asking her to watch and correct. It felt easier, holding the needles and yarn in the same way she did.

"What on Earth are you doing?" asked my instructor, watching me purl[1] in our second or third lesson. "That's totally wrong, I've never seen someone knit like that." For several minutes she inspected my work, stretching the fabric and turning it this way and that, before admitting that, whatever I was doing, it was producing the correct stitch.

*

The purl is one of only two knitting stitches: knit, purl. To transform a skein of yarn into a piece of fabric, the knit stitch is enough, though comfort with both stitches is necessary if you want to graduate beyond "unwearable first scarf" territory. From those two stitches comes everything: stockinette

---

[1] How to purl, according to me: place the tip of the right needle beneath the working yarn. Slide the tip of the right needle into the first stitch on the left needle, from the right. Waggle the right needle around in some kind of way so that when you move the stitch onto the right-hand needle, surprise! It's a purl.

stitch, cables running up the arm of a sweater, the turn of a sock's heel, complex lacework with glinting beads nestled into the stitches, blankets spiraling outward from a center pinhole tugged shut when the project is complete.

In my first knitting lessons, my instructor showed us how the purl stitch had a bump, while the knit stitch was smooth. For months, though, they looked the same to me as I knitted—how could anyone see the bump nestled beneath their needle? It was only when I looked at a length of knitting that I could distinguish between the two stitches. "Is this the knit side or the purl side?" I would ask my mother when I lost my place in a pattern, desperate to acquire her skill—to look at a piece of knitting and understand, immediately, how it had been put together.

*

As my instructor's response to my knitting style may have indicated, there's a tension between English and continental knitters. Both regard themselves as superior, and frequently they cannot offer useful guidance to knitters working in the other style. My grandmother, who has never paid much attention to me and recently complained to her children that she had only ever wished someone would name a baby after her (I am named after her), frequently praises the fact that I am a continental knitter. So graceful, such even tension! I don't tell her, though, that I do occasionally knit in the English style. When I'm working on a fair isle sweater, or anything that requires working multiple colors of yarn, I will purl like the American I am.

*

After that first bad scarf, I discovered that the secret to good knitting is good yarn. Spend $20 or $30 on a skein of yarn and, as long as you're decent and make smart design choices (no combining complex cable patterns with complex color-shifting yarns, which will result in a sludgy mess) you'll end up with a good-looking piece of knitwear. I made a cowl that was soft and wearable. I made a lacy beanie that, for a year, I wore everywhere. "I made it!" I exclaimed whenever someone complimented the hat. I made a short-sleeved sweater, with frequent assists from my mother, that fit.

My next discovery was that, when you begin wearing your own knitting into the world, people will frequently suggest you monetize your hobby. I can usually dismiss these suggestions on purely logistical terms—I can't sell clothing based on a pattern I didn't design; the yarn alone costs more than people would pay for the finished object—but the truth is that knitting for profit seems like no fun. The part of knitting I least enjoy is the finishing, when I soak and shape my knitwear: pinning a baby blanket to a blocking board, or pulling a damp hat onto my towel-covered head. What I like is the knitting itself, feeling the yarn run between my fingers, watching a pattern's gradual emergence from my metal needles. It's almost absurd, that with a skein of yarn and two sticks I can produce a hat that only a fellow knitter will recognize as homemade. Why ruin that with money?

*

As a new knitter, I listened in horror as more experienced knitters talked about "frogging" projects, as my mother described unraveling a sweater (an entire sweater!) as it neared completion, having realized she didn't like the design. After unraveling, she soaked the yarn to remove its kinks; when it was dry, she wound the yarn into fresh skeins, ready for use in a new project. Eventually, I realized that I, too, could abandon a project when it bored me or I didn't like the look of things— that there was no shame in saying, "Nope, this isn't working."

Six months ago, though, I skipped a yarnover while working on the yoke of a sweater. I was holding a strand of mohair along with my main yarn, which would make the finished sweater hazy, ethereal, and incomprehensibly soft. By the time I realized my mistake, I had knitted fully around the sweater. I tried to retrace my steps, backing up two hundred stitches, undoing everything I had done between the mistake and my discovery of the mistake; but the mohair caught on itself and it was impossible to untangle the lacework. I picked down to the error and worked out a partial fix, which resulted in the correct number of stitches on my needle but didn't look right. I knitted on, but every time I saw the error I put the sweater down.

I had already worked a couple weeks on the sweater and was halfway through the most annoying part of the project. I had spent almost $200 on the yarn and worried I didn't have enough to start over. No one but me would notice the error; even if I pointed it out, most people wouldn't be able to see the mistake. But—I would notice, and for six months I left the project sealed in its plastic bag, annoyed every time I saw or thought of it.

The solution was obvious, of course. You know what it is. I'd always known what it was. One night last week I pulled my needles from the yarn. I cut the yoke into strips to feed to my compost bin. I weighed the remaining yarn and there was, as there'd always been, enough to start over.

THE SLOG ITSELF
Tasha Coryell

There is a picture of a man who pooped himself during a half marathon—Mikael Ekvall—that makes the rounds online every so often. People share the picture with glee, saying, "this is why I don't run." In a 2015 article about the poop runner, *Gawker* labeled the image as a "demotivational poster," a type of meme meant to dash ambitions and make fun of achievers.

Running, more than any other physical activity, attracts this particular type of ire. There is a cultural and commercial industry surrounding the hatred of running including t-shirts that say things like "If I'm running, please catch whatever is chasing me" and "0.0 miles" car magnets making fun of the "26.2" magnets popularized by marathon runners.

It could be argued that this hatred is correlated with a type of misery that is specific to running. After all, running includes minutes to hours of intensive cardio that is both physically and mentally difficult. Running, as exemplified by Mikael Ekvall, can cause gastrointestinal distress as well as a myriad of other injuries. In my time running, I've suffered through ankle pain, an IT band injury, piriformis syndrome that made sitting down painful, and a calf strain that sidelined me for months and was only treatable with dry needling, which is a procedure where a physical therapist sticks a series of needles into your muscle. Even when I'm at my physical peak, running can be immensely uncomfortable due to weather, soreness, or the sheer amount of effort it takes to make any kind of improvements to speed. When I ran my first 10k, I told my brother—former captain of his high school cross country and track teams—that I didn't care how long it took me, I just wanted to feel good while doing it and he said, "Oh, you're going to feel horrible the entire time." Recovery from running can also be painful. After my first marathon, I was so sore that I struggled to step up onto a curb when going out to eat after the race. The muscles on my legs become so tight and knotted that when they cramp up during stretches, it comes as a relief. This type of pain is endemic to the sport. Anyone who runs enough is likely to eventually encounter an injury of some kind and most avid runners become virtual experts in the various aggravations of the legs and how to treat them.

I suspect, however, that the reason running is so hated is because most people have had at least some experience in it, regardless of their athletic prowess. Until 2013, students in U.S. public schools had to participate in the Presidential Fitness Test, which included a one-mile endurance run. More than any other activity in gym class, the mile run made clear who the athletic kids were and who, like me, were members of the theater club and spent hours watching television. The good runners finished quickly and watched as the rest of us lapsed into walking and traipsed around the track for what felt like endless loops. It was so humiliating that I still remember the name—*Nick*—of the kid that made fun of the way that I ran in junior high. My senior year of high school I asked Nick about this incident and he said, "Oh, I probably had a crush on you," waving away something that had traumatized me for years. More recently, 5ks have grown in popularity and include themes that are meant to appeal to people who don't conventionally think of themselves as runners such as the Color Run, where participants are sprayed with a variety of paint colors or the Krispy Kreme Challenge, which involves speed eating a dozen donuts at the halfway point of the race. I did several of these themed 5ks in in high school with a friend that was a much better runner than I was. I spent a lot of my free time walking and thus never trained for these events, thinking that I could easily walk three miles, how hard could it be to run? As it turns out, walking does not translate well to running and I left the events so sore that I had to spend the rest of the day on the couch.

In addition to being forced into running in school, running is often touted as the most accessible exercise because it doesn't require any equipment. If someone is out of shape and wants to get in shape, all they need to do is go out their front door, the line goes. Any experienced runner can explain the fallacy of this logic. Quality running shoes are expensive and cheap shoes can lead to injury, which comes with its own costs. My own shoes cost over a hundred dollars and that doesn't include the special inserts that I purchase. I also wear moisture-wicking clothes, socks that ward off blisters, a GPS watch, and headphones. On any given run, my outfit is more expensive than my nicest outfit that I wear to work. After I injured my IT band several years ago, I started doing strength training with a personal trainer that adds an additional cost per month. Running also requires access to safe sidewalks or trails, which can be difficult to find in a car-obsessed culture. My usual running route involves crossing busy streets and train tracks and I've almost be hit by distracted drivers on several occasions. Races can be incredibly expensive and may require travel depending on where a person lives. On top of all of that, running takes a lot of time, which many people cannot afford.

This fallacy about accessibility causes some people to feel guilty for their own lack of running prowess ("I'm so bad at running!") and other people to feel confident that they would be excellent runners if only they dedicated their time to it ("someday I'm going to run a marathon"). While the majority of people, myself included, will never become expert runners, it's likely that most people could improve if the time and cost barriers were removed and they had help from actual running coaches rather than being told to "just go outside." I'm not sure the likelihood of someone actually running a marathon if they have a stated, distant goal of doing so, but I'm guessing the number of people who successfully complete a marathon is significantly lower than the number of people who want to complete a marathon. In other words, there are plenty of people that don't run because they have significant barriers that make running difficult and then there are people that don't run because they don't actually want to run, they just conceptually like the notion of themselves as runners.

There are, of course, many people who consistently run and even enjoy running. Some rationalize this behavior through the notion of a "runner's high," which refers to feelings of euphoria that a runner may feel during or after a run. I've talked to numerous people who claim that they don't experience a runner's high. I can't speak for those people, but it took me quite a long time before I felt anything close to what I would describe as a runner's high. I first had to get over my lack of cardio fitness in order to become capable of running long enough. Now, I regularly experience a gentle buzz of satisfaction when I complete a run, a sensation that is tempered by those days when run doesn't go as planned and I return home irritated. This still leaves the question of why I continued to run before I experienced a runner's high and why I do runs that are more likely to cause misery than joy.

I first started running because I wanted to be a particular type of person. I had just come back from a year of teaching English in Austria where I experienced a series of heartbreaks, both romantic and otherwise, and was also recovering from foot pain caused by shoes that were too small that made it difficult to walk. I wanted to physically and mentally become the type of person that no one would want to break up with, someone in charge of their own emotional state and not left vulnerable to boys who did or did not text back. I know now that it's stupid to run for weight loss or in attempts to achieve a particular type of body. It's true that many runners are thin, but there are runners of a multitude of body types and running on its own does not inherently mean weight loss. In fact, I usually gain weight while training for marathons. I never transformed into the runner of my dreams, the kind featured in a Nike commercial who runs in slick gear as rain bounces off her skin. What I did discover is that there is joy in the slog.

The slog is waking up at 5am to go running while everyone else is still sleeping. The slog is running when it is too hot or too cold. The slog is running through the rain. The slog is getting stopped by a train and waiting by the train tracks until it passes. The slog is getting passed by people that are younger and better than you have any hope to be. The slog is competing in a race and not getting the time that you wanted. For some people, the slog is running every day and for others it's running only on weekends. The slog is stopping to use a porta potty on the side of the trail. The slog is running on a hotel treadmill, through parking lots and unpaved roads. The slog is finishing your run and still having another mile until you're home because you miscalculated the distance. Sometimes the slog means stopping, means tending to injury, means procrastinating before you get started. The slog is not related to movement alone.

Not everyone likes the slog and that's okay. There is no reason that everyone has to run and there is no moral purity in suffering. There are lots of exercises that provide the same physical and mental benefits as running without the sheen of misery that running carries with it. It's fine to do something else. However, there are people, like me, that relish the slog.

My dad also used to run and he told me once that he preferred training over running races. I didn't get it then. Wasn't running races the whole point? I do experience a sense of victory when crossing the finish line, listening to people cheer, and putting that medal around my neck. The problem is that races are ephemeral. It's an accomplishment for a week or two as I rest my legs and then I'm back in the slog. There are people who run races nearly constantly, but I know that my body would never hold up to that strain. For me, it's about day-to-day. The small rituals that make up my running practice, that have become so ingrained in my life that they are virtually indistinguishable from who I am. To slog through the humidity, even on the days I don't want to or lack inspiration.

Following his poop incident, a reporter asked Mikael Ekvall why he continued as shit streamed down his legs and he replied, "If you quit once, it's easy to do it again and again and again. It becomes a habit." I've read numerous books about running and nothing has stuck more than this. I like activities that other people find tedious, the type of activity that requires commitment day after day. I'm not a naturally gifted runner—my hips are too wide and my glutes too weak—and I will never be the type of person that wins races though I occasionally place in my age group. I don't need to professionalize all of my hobbies or only partake in things where I am the best. It's enough that I wake up in the morning and decide, yes, I will do this thing that is sometimes kind of miserable and sometimes kind of wonderful.

BIOS & NOTES

James Brubaker is the author of *We Are Ghost Lit, The Taxidermist's Catalog, Black Magic Death Sphere: (science) fictions, Liner Notes*, and *Pilot Season*. He teaches writing and runs the University Press at Southeast Missouri State University. He owns far too many records. His favorite current record store is Planet Score in St. Louis. His favorite of all time was Encore Records in Ann Arbor at its old location.

I don't write many essays. This isn't because I don't enjoy writing them, but because I don't tend to think I have anything interesting to say. Most of the essays I've written over the years (excluding reviews) have been for TheRS500 *or* wig-wag, *and maybe roughly a third of those I agreed to write at the last minute when the editor was in a pinch, and roughly sixty-percent of them blurred the boundaries between fiction and essay to the point I'm not even sure they were really even essays. My point: prior to writing "About that Time I Sold My Copies of the First Three American Analog Set Records When I Really, Truly Shouldn't Have, and Have Regretted it Ever Since," I'd intentionally written maybe only five essays that I plotted out ahead of time, and then actually wrote. That's probably for the best because most of the ideas I have for essays wind up being incredibly niche. Over the course of my life, I've learned to read the blank stares on friends and loved one's faces when I start to "go deep" into some subject matter about which I'm very excited, but which most people find somewhat boring. That is to say, I've learned when to taper off and change the subject. And it's those blank-stare producing deep dives that end up accounting for most of the essays I wind up wanting to write, and, well, I know there just isn't going to be a ton of interest in any of them: I want to write about ob-*

scure CD-R tour only EPs, limited to thirty copies, released by Fred Thomas in 2002; I want to write about 45s released by Jeremy Apland's short-lived punk bands in the late 90s Dayton, Ohio punk/indie/emo scene; I want to write about forgotten television shows that aired only four episodes, and exquisite novels that never found an audience, and films that were never released on home video and still aren't streaming; and of course, before I even knew Autofocus would be publishing a volume of essays about novel writing that didn't mention novel writing, I wanted to write an essay about collecting records that would double as an essay about writing fiction. I'd been thinking a lot about my record collection, and how my approach to collecting had changed over the years, and then I realized that my collecting habits were evolving parallel to my approach to writing, and there it was, a fun and exciting essay idea that I'd probably never write because the intersection of records and writing seemed a little too specific to my own interests to find a home. But then I saw the call for essays for this book, and here we are. The only other thing I want to add is this: the day that I found out my essay would appear in this book, Chicago-based label The Numero Group announced they'd be reissuing the first three American Analog Set LPs on vinyl, and I'm pretty excited about that.

Ashleigh Catibog-Abraham is a writer based in Toronto. Her work has been featured in *Empyrean Literary Magazine* and *Last Leaves Magazine*. When she's not writing, she's watching movies and making TikToks about watching movies. IG @ashleighcatabe | TikTok @ashsquickiereviews & @ashwritesstuff

This piece was written during a very dark time in my postpartum journey. I had given birth and it was supposed to be the happiest time of my life. When I was writing this piece, my child was nearing a year old and I felt at a complete loss because it seemed that I couldn't do anything right. I also was very hesitant to seek help about how I was feeling, fearing that it would be perceived as weakness or complaining.

I didn't feel like the mother my child deserved. I wanted to be able to move the moon and stars for her, but there were days when I could barely get out of bed to take a shower.

I wrote this to remind myself that I had done something incredible, and it was not meant to be easy. I shouldn't have to feel guilty when things are difficult, especially when I am doing the best I can. Parenthood changes you in a lot of ways, I can only hope that I've been changed for the better. My daughter had breathed new life into me, she has given me a new purpose to keep moving forward.

Katharine Coldiron is the author of a novella, *Ceremonials*, and a collection of criticism, *Junk Film*. Her essays and reviews have appeared in *Conjunctions, the Washington Post, LARB, the Kenyon Review, the Offing*, and many other places. Find her at kcoldiron.com or on Twitter @ferrifrigida.

Since I wrote the sentence "I have learned that a surprising number of people do not follow the directions," I've thought about it nearly every day. The irony of that sentence appearing in this book is that there are almost no universally useful directions on how to write. (I admit I was thinking of my submissions queue when I wrote it; if you're submitting something to a magazine, read the damn directions.) Elmore Leonard says to try to leave out the parts that readers tend to skip, and that has stood me in good stead in every kind of writing I've ever done. All else is subjective.

Tasha Coryell received her MFA and PhD from the University of Alabama, during which she ran three marathons, a bunch of half marathons, and wrote several books, most of which will never be published. Her book of short stories, *Hungry People*, was published by Split/Lip Press in 2018 and her debut novel, *Love Letters to a Serial Killer*, is coming out in 2024.

I recently completed a PhD in Composition and Rhetoric, a field that I enjoy, but one that is distinctly different from creative writing. Before I started the program, I worried that I would stop writing fiction, an activity that has been a constant for me since I was a kid. Instead, doing academic work reminded me how much fucking fun it is to write a novel. I continued to write novels through coursework and my dissertation, carving out fifteen-minute chunks of time to work on projects that I wasn't sure would ever get published or be read by anyone aside from myself. I got confused when I saw people complain about writing and realized that a lot of the misery wasn't related to writing itself, but despair over publication or lack thereof. While I understand why publication is important, writing a novel takes so long that it needs to be about more than the end goal. There needs to be some level of joy in the simple act of sitting down at the computer and typing some words.

In addition to writing nearly every day, I also run, and these feel like linked activities to me. Months of work go into training for a race and come race day, the majority of runners don't accomplish anything extraordinary. This isn't a failure on their part. Most people don't start training for a marathon with the expectation that they're going to finish in first place and I don't think that the primary pleasure in writing should stem from publication alone. Doing something because you want to do it is a good enough reason. Showing up consistently is something to be proud of regardless of the end result. I have bad runs just as I have bad writing days, but both activities are still thrilling. I do it because I love to do it and I think that love is a part of the process just as much or more than any understanding of plot or convention.

Siân Griffiths lives in Ogden, Utah, where she serves as a Professor of English and Creative Writing at Weber State University. Her work has appeared in *Colorado Review, The Georgia Review, Prairie Schooner, American Short Fiction*, and *Booth* among many other publications. She is the author of the novels *Borrowed Horses* and

Scrapple and the short fiction chapbook *The Heart Keeps Faulty Time*, and her essay collection *The Sum of Her Parts* is newly out from University of Georgia Press. Currently, she reads fiction as part of the editorial team at *Barrelhouse*. For more information, please visit sbgriffiths.com

Writing and riding have long been my twin obsessions. For most of my life, I've ridden as much as I could afford. As a child, this meant a weekly lesson but no horse. When I was older, I worked tedious, soul-crushing hours at Hardees, trying to ignore my boss's casual sexual harassment, so that I could keep up the weekly lessons. After college, I bought my first horse with a personal loan, using my beat-up old car as collateral. I traded barn chores for a back bedroom rather than an apartment for myself so my horse could have a home. I wrote my first novel when that horse retired, dedicating it to him. The writing was a way to salve the wound that not riding created as I continued to pay pasture board—an expense that my grad school stipend was not made to cover. My husband once said that, rather than horses, I should take up crack cocaine because it would be cheaper and bring more reliable joy. He was and was not joking. Perhaps riding is an addiction, but it's one I'll stand by.

The thing is, riding reveals truths to me in a way that nothing else does. Horses have taught me about grace and about joy. They have also taught me about acceptance. I am not the rider I want to be, in spite of all my lessons and practice and dedication, but I inch closer. The striving is the point. This is true for being a writer as well, and when Aaron Burch put out the call for this anthology, I knew that I needed to find expression for the ways the wordless communication with a horse and the word-bound communication of a novel were weirdly similar pursuits.

Abby Harding writes about the difficulty of being human through poetry, fiction, and creative nonfiction. She lives in central Illinois with three children, a husband, two cats, a guinea pig, and six chickens. You can find more of her work and links to her socials at abbyharding.com.

This essay surprised me. I had no idea when I started writing it how many correlations I could draw between the path I took to gardening and the process of becoming a writer. Just like my dreams of having a garden, I dreamed of being a writer from a young age, but I wanted it the same way I wanted that garden: handed to me without too much effort. I feared failure and "wasting" time on projects that wouldn't be perfect on the first try, so I simply never started. A few years ago, after an enlightening conversation with friends, I realized that the only difference between an Aspiring Writer and a Real Writer is which one sits down and puts words on a page. So, I began to do just that. This essay hints at some of the lessons I've learned since: most of writing is the process, not the result, but nothing beats the feeling of holding your words in your hands; a dose of humility and a teachable spirit are your allies; and good writers start as good readers, so read accordingly.

Hattie Jean Hayes is a writer and comedian, originally from a small town in Missouri, who now lives in New York. Her work has appeared in *The Ex-Puritan, Hell Is Real, Janus Literary, HAD,* and others. Her writing has been nominated for the Pushcart Prize and Best of the Net. Hattie completed a SAFTA residency in September 2022, has a poetry chapbook forthcoming from Bullshit Lit in summer 2023, and is revising her first novel. Please read her newsletter (which is ½ poetry, ½ blog) and visit hattiehayes.com whenever you feel like it.

I labeled the summer of 2019 my "dirtbag summer" because I was unemployed / underemployed / drinking warm champagne on the train by myself a lot. Maybe that sounds glamorous but it was mostly gross. I wrote a different essay about that little meltdown, called How to Heal a Sunburn, which was published in The Ex-Puritan. But my dirtbag era ended in August 2019, when I took the bad temp job you read about in this anthology.

I was there until February 2020. My parents live in Missouri and I had scheduled time off because I was flying home to throw their seventh-anniversary party (they were married on Leap Day). Before I left for my (unpaid) time off, I walked into work to overhear the women I worked with laughing, loudly, at a racial slur one of them had used to spice up her daily breakfast of gossip. During my lunch break, I called the temp agency and asked to be placed somewhere else when I came back from my visit home. We were in the middle of planning a major international conference, which was supposed to be held March 23 – 27, 2020, but I quit anyway. It was a good move.

My trip to Missouri was perfect. Even though I was going back to New York City and unemployment after the weekend, I felt totally calm, with no sense of dread. And I didn't know it at the time, but that anniversary party would be the last time much of my extended family would ever be together.

I came back to New York. The next week, I began working from home for a new company. In September 2020, I finally wrote down everything that had come to life in the margins of that horrible temp job. I finished the first draft of my novel in eight days.

Ruth Joffre is the author of the story collection *Night Beast*. Her work has been shortlisted for the Creative Capital Awards, longlisted for The Story Prize, and supported by residencies at the Virginia Center for the Creative Arts, Lighthouse Works, The Arctic Circle, and the Whiteley Center. Her writing has appeared or is forthcoming in more than 50 publications, including *Lightspeed, Pleiades, Fantasy, khōréō, The Florida Review Online, Kenyon Review, Reckoning, Wigleaf,* and the anthologies *Best Microfiction 2021* & *2022*. A graduate of Cornell University and the Iowa Writers' Workshop, Ruth served as the 2020-2022 Prose Writer-in-Residence at Hugo House and as a Visiting Writer at University of Washington Bothell in 2023.

How fascinating to return to this essay now, having left the job mentioned in the first section and moved from the Pacific Northwest to Missouri. This piece was born out of the same exhaustion and wonder that gave rise to my birding obsession, of the desire to have something—anything—to expand the joy in my life amidst the pandemic and that demanding 9 to 5. In many ways, this essay is a love letter to one of the things that kept me going. It's also a kind of elegy, because I entered birding at a particularly fraught time, with climate change pushing many species to the brink. As a birder (and one who began in earnest while traveling), I'm acutely aware of the fact that every time I see a bird might be the last time. As a writer, I think there's a lesson here about identifying and seizing moments of joy so they can sustain you for the work ahead.

Shane Kowalski lives in Pennsylvania. He teaches creative writing at Ursinus College. He is the author of *Small Moods* (Future Tense Books).

I worked for the post office from 2019 through 2022, which included the start of a global pandemic and a particularly contentious election year. People, when you saw them, became stranger over the course of months. Almost every day I'd think, I should write about this. But then when I got home, I found that I couldn't. I jotted down the facts of things that had happened but couldn't seem to tease out the narrative elements—the interesting stuff that makes a story that happens to you into a story that you tell to other people.

It was too real and fresh. I started to think that maybe if I found a way to write the stories as they were happening, that somehow, I would wreck my life, become a character in it, and be forced into whatever absurd and bureaucratic fate tomorrow held. So, I decided to let the stuff keep happening to me. And I resolved to just write it later.

While working there, I mostly thought of how similar the work of the post office is to the work of writing. They both have their rituals and habits. Both solitary in practice yet communal in effect. I thought about how there's so much work we don't see that goes into the simple pleasure of receiving a letter from a friend or reading a book by a stranger. It was this absence that drove the writing of this piece.

Kevin Maloney is the author of *The Red-Headed Pilgrim, Cult of Loretta,* and the forthcoming story collection *Horse Girl Fever.* His writing has appeared in *HAD, Barrelhouse, Green Mountains Review,* and a number of other journals and anthologies. He lives in Portland, Oregon with his wife Aubrey.

2008 was a huge year for me. I'd been divorced three years, had narrowly avoided getting married again, only to find myself single for the first time in a decade. I was 31 years old. I'd just quit smoking. I quit drinking for almost a year. And I was back in Portland, Oregon, my hometown—a city which I'd tried to flee from my whole life, but which now was a destination for artists, most of them five, six years younger than me. Everybody was making something. I felt close to them and totally different than them. They worked at coffee shops and bars; I worked at a marketing-PR firm. They were beautifully carefree; I had a six-year-old child. But I knew that this was my chance to become the artist I'd always wanted to be. A disciplined one. I started writing and painting like they were my real jobs, the marketing-PR work an annoying distraction. I wrote every Saturday and Sunday morning. I wrote at work when it was slow. I painted in the evenings. For the first time in my life, I really felt like myself.

Then something unexpected happened—my heart, which had been battered again and again during a long, unhappy marriage, burst wide open, and I felt immensely connected with the world around me. I was developing the Habit of Art (as Flannery O'Connor calls it). I looked at people and noticed their faces and felt constantly on the verge of tears. My inner world of suffering collapsed and suddenly I saw suffering in people and trees and squirrels and birds. I saw beauty and pain all around me. I became curious. I realized that this was the other half of being an artist—not just the discipline of sitting down (or standing) every day to make art, but being openhearted and inquisitive about the world. Constantly stripping away the bullshit and learning to really see. This essay is my attempt to convey the sense of wonder I discovered in 2008, that I keep trying to uncover again and again.

Scott Mitchel May is a writer living in Madison, WI. He was the winner of the 2019 UW-Madison Writers' Institute Poem or Page Competition in the category of literary fiction, and his unpublished novel, *Bridgeport Nowhere*, was shortlisted for the 2022 Santa Fe Writers' Project Literary Award. His debut novel, *Breakneck: or it happened once in America*, was published by Anxiety Press in April 2023. He is also the author of the novelette, *All Burn Down*, forthcoming in October 2023 from Emerge Press, and his second novel, *Awful People: a ghost story*, is coming in early 2024 from Death of Print Books. He holds a GED from the Wisconsin Department of Public Instruction and a BS in English Literature from Edgewood College. He tweets @smitchelmay.

I saw the submission call on Twitter, thought that it sounded like fun, and then thought that I didn't have anything I wanted to write for it. Or, rather, I did, but that essay writing isn't my thing. But the trigger was primed. The idea that it would be fun for me to write an essay about how to write a novel that never mentioned how to write a novel was in my head and it felt a certain way I recognized. It felt like I would just think and think and think about it until I wrote the fucking thing. Which I did, in one sitting, the day before submissions opened.

This is how I write novels. Something sticks in my head that I think I'd have a lot of fun writing and then I think and think and think about it, sometimes for years as I'm writing something else, something else I thought would be fun to write about, and then, finally, when the issue is forced, I sit down and I write the fucking thing.

Usually, one hour at a time and with no outline. I've been doing this almost every single day for the last nine years. The only reason I do it is that I think it's really fun. The idea of supporting myself with the fun parts of writing is so sort of unattainable seeming that to do it for any other reason than I truly enjoy writing long-ass complicated narratives without any roadmap seems foolish. So, I guess, remember that it's creative writing, it's supposed to be fun.

Mitchell Nobis is a writer and K-12 public school teacher in Metro Detroit. His fiction has appeared in *Porcupine Literary, Flyover Country, and Rejection Letters and his poetry in HAD, Whale Road Review, The Night Heron Barks*, and more. He also hosts the Wednesday Night Sessions reading series and may someday finish his basketball novel. Find him at mitchnobis.com, on Twitter (and others) at @MitchNobis, or falling apart on a basketball court in one Detroit suburb or another.

I tend to see everything through basketball metaphors. When I teach writing, I say daily informal writing is like "shooting free throws every day." When my wife or I have to miss our kids' bedtime routine, we say the one at home is "running a zone defense." When four other teachers and I started co-authoring a book on how to teach essay writing, we talked about who would be "the point guard" of the project. (I honestly don't know what else to call that role. What do MBA people put on their resumes when they lead a project? Never mind—don't answer that. I don't want to know, and besides, it's a point guard.)
You can never master writing or basketball. There is always a next level. Both fields have greats, but none ever mastered it. It looks to you and me like they did, but even Toni Morrison said in interviews that she felt like she still failed all the time and was just editing to make it better, not perfect. Maybe that's why writing and basketball are congruent in my mind. Both are about pursuit, and excellence or achievement can be interpreted in thousands of ways.

When I saw the call for this anthology, my first thought was, "Mitch you hoser, you can't write about this—you've spent over a decade on a novel and haven't finished it." My second thought was, "You never made the NBA either, but you keep playing basketball." That's my problem—I lost a rec league game last night, and instead of realizing I'm too old and too slow and just not talented enough to win the big game, I'll be right back there next week, just like I'll keep chipping away at my novel (or novels, really) because what else am I going to do, not write? Please. Shooters gotta shoot.

Abigail Oswald can be found at the movie theater in at least one parallel universe at any given time. Her writing has appeared or is forthcoming in *Best Microfiction, Wigleaf, DIAGRAM, Split Lip, The Rumpus*, and elsewhere. She holds an MFA from Sarah Lawrence College and currently lives in Connecticut. More online at abigailwashere.com.

I wrote this essay the summer that Top Gun: Maverick *was released in theaters, which was my first Tom Cruise movie on the big screen since finishing his catalog during the pandemic. In this era of forever sequels and instantaneous reboots, something intrigued me about the thirty-six-year gap between the first film and the continuation of its story. I find comfort in the idea that while I'm out in the world living my life, these characters we know and love are living theirs, too. Maverick didn't cease to exist at the end of* Top Gun; *he's been flying planes and talking back and getting older. And maybe that's all writing ever is, really—a brief window into a whole sprawling existence, whether it's real or imagined. It confirmed my belief that some stories are simply meant to be told, even if the timeline is a bit different than what we might first expect.*

e rathke writes about books and games at radicaledward.substack. com. A finalist for the 2022 Baen Fantasy Adventure Award, he is the author of *Glossolalia, Howl, The Shattered Stars,* and several other forthcoming novellas. His short fiction appears in *Queer Tales of Monumental Invention, Mysterion Magazine, Shoreline of Infinity,* and elsewhere.

I never learned how to write. Not really. I didn't get an English or Creative Writing degree or an MFA. Never read any books on the craft of writing or even Stephen King's On Writing, *which seems to be a book everyone's read.*

What I did do was read and read and read some more and then take my own fumbling attempts at putting words together. Much of it has been by instinct and experimentation and compulsion, which has often led me down dark alleys leading nowhere, but has also led me to wondrous new worlds I hadn't anticipated—that I could not have anticipated or planned.

I don't remember when I learned to cook, but I suppose I've always been tinkering around in the kitchen. While I never had a cooking teacher, I did have a tongue and a mouth full of teeth, so eating came quite naturally, if you can believe it. Taste—glorious taste—and instinct and experimentation has been my guide in the kitchen, and I've always felt that preparing food is, perhaps, the purest form of art: temporary, pleasurable, for others, but enriching myself.

And it's the lessons I've learned in the kitchen that have taught me most about fiction.

Amie Souza Reilly lives in Connecticut where she is an Instructor and Writer in Residence at Sacred Heart University. Her work has appeared in *Wigleaf, Atticus Review, The Chestnut Review, Smoke-Long Quarterly* and elsewhere, and has also appeared on *Wigleaf's* Top 50 and been nominated for Best of the Net. Her collection of essays *My Animal Body, My Animal Language* is forthcoming with Wilfred Laurier University Press.

I saw the call for essays for this project right around the same time I hit the one-year mark of submitting—and receiving rejections for—a manuscript I'd finished. It was also the first summer without our beloved dog, who'd died on Valentine's Day. We were in our second pandemic year. What I am saying is, when I wrote this, I teetered at the edge of despair.

I'd been thinking a lot about staying and leaving. The rejections I'd received were mostly kind and supportive, so I couldn't figure out whether to start over or just keep trying. Our dog was gone but her hair remained threaded into the couch and every single one of my socks. We live in a world filled with loss and yet, tulips.

To write about laundry as writing (or writing as laundry?) became another way of thinking about this same opposition. Laundry, like writing, is a kind of staying and leaving, an inevitable cycle of removing what we leave behind. This essay feels like a lot of little metaphors nested inside an overarching one. Writing, like laundry, reveals our unique vulnerabilities. We write and do laundry in domestic spaces, places of kept secrets and unseen work. We use tools for laundry and we use tools for writing and some function better than others. Both are a process. Clothes are writing, the washing of them is writing. Lost socks of unwritten ideas. Mistakes, regrets, memories.

Kirsten Reneau received her MFA from the University of New Orleans. She has been nominated for several awards and won a couple. Her debut collection *Sensitive Creatures* will be out with Belle Point Press in 2024.

Every road leading from my childhood home is a backroad, meaning I learned how to drive on dirt roads, blind curves, and behind coal trucks. It is a very intimate knowledge. I recently had to go home and drive my partner to the city and I got to drive those same roads again. It made me start to think: how do you share what you did not realize you knew so well?

Since I could remember being a person, I have always wanted to write. Not to get self-righteous about it, but I believe that to write is to participate in a divine act of creation. It can be frustrating. It takes practice. But there is no better feeling on earth than when you are writing and you can feel where you have gone merge with where you are going and it all feels just right.

Ellen Rhudy lives in Philadelphia. She has an MFA from The Ohio State University, and her fiction has appeared in journals including *The Cincinnati Review, Story,* and *The Florida Review.*

Glancing back at this essay's timeline, I begin to suspect my target audience was me. I drafted the essay when I was starting the fourth draft of my novel, sure that this time I was going to get it right. When Aaron accepted the essay, I had just deleted the first half of the fourth draft of the novel and begun the fun task of writing 50,000 mostly new words I was pretty sure I would also eventually dispose of. By the time I'm holding this anthology, I'll be starting another rewrite. It's comforting to remind myself that, like the sweater I haven't yet begun to reknit, the novel is always waiting for me and will eventually exist, though possibly in a form I am not yet able to anticipate.

Donald Ryan is the author of *Don Bronco's (Working Title) Shell* from Malarkey Books. Other works have appeared in *Fiction Southeast, Reckon Review, The Daily Drunk, The Lumiere Review,* and elsewhere. Donald Ryan solely exists online dot com and on Twitter at dryanswords.

And now for dessert: a mixed berry mousse paired with a fresh and refreshing strawberry basil digestif—because my kid loves berries. Like, I've never had so many clear clam cases stacked in the fridge. Blueberries. Blackberries. All berries. And especially strawberries. But with strawberries comes the question of the ass-end and what to do with it.

Now, I'm not great at it, and hell, most of the time I'm not even that good, but I do try to cut down on food waste. Something ingrained from my restaurant days, watching how much gets thrown out by the hour from the front and back of house. There's no poetry in it, for the plants and animals that gave their lives. So I'll either chop around the stem, save up the bits, then mix them in a food processor with a handful of other berries (blend, then), sugar, and a single egg white, then blend (again) till it triples in size. Or, I'll soak the end, stem and all, in vodka with basil (and a cardamon pod if I'm feeling sassy) for a day or two, until the color drains from the scraps and into the liquor. Strain this and mix over ice with some sort of squeezed citrus (lemons, grapefruits, or oranges all do quite nicely) and soda water. Simple, crisp, and helps to remind me "not a right fit" one place does not mean it can't be a treat someplace else. Plus, my kid loves it—not even two and already all about that stiff, after-dinner drink.

Emma Sloley's fiction and creative non-fiction has appeared in *Catapult, Literary Hub, Joyland, The Common, CRAFT,* and the *Masters' Review Anthology,* among many others. She is a MacDowell fellow and Bread Loaf scholar, and her debut novel, *Disaster's Children,* was published by Little A books in 2019. Her second novel is forthcoming from Flatiron. Born in Australia, Emma now divides her time between California and the city of Mérida, Mexico.

While I have yet to be asked the classic book tour audience question "Where do your story ideas come from?" I've often pondered what my response would be. (Why yes, I do squander most of my rich interior life manifesting future scenarios in which I'm a writer of note and audiences are clamoring for my craft wisdom.) My essay here is a kind of answer. A disproportionate number of story ideas come to me not at my desk or in the sacred silence of a library or on long soulful walks in the woods or any other location you might reasonably expect a writer to be coming up with ideas, but in nail bars, hair salons, and other clamorous places dedicated to the Sisyphean task of self-beautification.

The seed for one of my favorite pieces of writing, a short story called "Sugartown," was born in the nail salon I mention in the essay. I was sitting in the chair, transfixed by the surreal show about cakes playing soundlessly on the big screens, and into that strange, banal space came a thought: imagine being someone who worked in a cake shop and you hated the smell of sugar. What an inconsequential but fun dilemma! On the heels of that thought came shuffling a person called Glory, a young woman dying of cancer who needed to pick up her last check from the cake shop at which she had worked up until her illness over- whelmed her.

I left the salon that day floating on the sugar-high of a new idea. If I hadn't decided I needed a manicure that day, would I even have met Glory? I doubt it. On opening the door to the salon I opened my brain to noticing weird things, and she slipped inside with me.

ABOUT THE EDITOR

Aaron Burch grew up in Tacoma, WA. He is the author of a novel, *Year of the Buffalo*; a memoir/literary analysis, *Stephen King's The Body*; a short story collection, *Backswing*; and a novella, *How to Predict the Weather*. He started the literary journal *Hobart*, which he edited for twenty years, and is currently the editor of *Short Story, Long* and the co-editor of *WAS* (Words & Sports) and *HAD*. He lives in Ann Arbor, MI and is online: on Twitter and Instagram at @aaron__burch, and the world wide web at aaronburch.net.

ɑ

Printed in the USA
CPSIA information can be obtained
at www.ICGtesting.com
CBHW021350230624
10507CB00002B/8

9 781957 392257